高职高专旅游专业"互联网+"创新规划教材

会展英语(第 2 版)

主　编　李世平　陈　颖
副主编　于海波
参　编　张兆敏　马宏伟

内 容 简 介

本书是在综合考虑会展行业实际需要和现有教学资源的基础上编写而成的。本书包括三大部分，共 15 个单元。第一部分为展前服务，包括：会展产业简介、广告、邀请、场馆选择、参加展览及展位装饰，共 6 个单元；第二部分为展中服务，包括：展台接待、销售展示、商务谈判、保险及签订合同，共 5 个单元；第三部分为展后服务，包括：处理投诉、撤展、展后联系及展会评估，共 4 个单元。每个单元的内容包括：学习目标、背景知识、热身活动、基础阅读、情景对话、常用口语、拓展阅读及实训项目等。

本书可作为高等院校会展专业及相关专业的教材，也可作为会展从业人员的业务参考书，还可作为非会展专业人士了解和学习会展英语知识、提高会展英语口语水平的实用教材。

图书在版编目(CIP)数据

会展英语 / 李世平，陈颖主编. —2 版. —北京：北京大学出版社，2020.6
高职高专旅游专业"互联网+"创新规划教材
ISBN 978-7-301-29289-1

Ⅰ.①会… Ⅱ.①李… ②陈… Ⅲ.①展览会－英语－高等职业教育－教材 Ⅳ.①G245

中国版本图书馆 CIP 数据核字（2018）第 034899 号

书　　　名	会展英语（第 2 版）
	HUIZHAN YINGYU(DI-ER-BAN)
著作责任者	李世平　陈　颖　主编
策划编辑	刘国明
责任编辑	翟　源
数字编辑	陈颖颖
标准书号	ISBN 978-7-301-29289-1
出版发行	北京大学出版社
地　　　址	北京市海淀区成府路 205 号　100871
网　　　址	http://www.pup.cn　新浪微博：@北京大学出版社
编辑部邮箱	pup6@pup.cn
总编室邮箱	zpup@pup.cn
电　　　话	邮购部 010-62752015　发行部 010-62750672　编辑部 010-62750667
印　刷　者	北京市科星印刷有限责任公司
经　销　者	新华书店
	787 毫米×1092 毫米　16 开本　13.5 印张　317 千字
	2013 年 4 月第 1 版
	2020 年 6 月第 2 版　2023 年 8 月第 4 次印刷
定　　　价	35.00 元

未经许可，不得以任何方式复制或抄袭本书之部分或全部内容。
版权所有，侵权必究
举报电话：010-62752024　电子信箱：fd@pup.pku.edu.cn
图书如有印装质量问题，请与出版部联系，电话：010-62756370

第 2 版前言
Preface

　　中国改革开放和社会主义现代化建设在二十大报告,"坚持和加强党的全面领导""坚持中国特色社会主义道路""坚持以人民为中心的发展思想""坚持深化改革开放""坚持发扬斗争精神"的指引下深入推进,中国正迈上全面建设社会主义现代化国家新征程。随着中国改革开放和国际化程度进一步深化,伴随着中国经济的崛起,中国会展业发展迅猛,规模和层次不断提高,社会效益和经济效益逐渐彰显,已经成为中国经济发展新的增长点,日益展现出强大的生命力和发展潜力,成为继旅游业之后又一个迅速崛起的朝阳产业,享有城市经济的"晴雨表"和"助推器"等美誉。

　　随着中国会展业的蓬勃发展,国际化、专业化步伐的加快,会展企业对具有国际竞争力的复合型会展人才的需求越来越旺盛,对会展人才的培养提出了更高的要求,也对会展英语教材提出了更高的要求。

　　本书就是在综合考虑会展行业实际需要和现有教学资源的基础上编写而成的。

　　本书的主编之一李世平老师从事英语教学与研究工作二十余年。早年澳大利亚留学的经历为她的教学与研究工作提供了独特的视角和理念,使其能够娴熟自如地熔东西方优秀的教育、教学理念和方法于一炉,对于如何培育会展英语人才、如何编著会展英语教材积累了丰富的经验和资料。

　　同以往的同类教材相比,本书具有以下特色。

　　(1) 职业特色鲜明,专业特色突出。本书按会展活动的工作流程来设计、编排内容,涵盖了会展业服务和管理的主要内容;将职业技能的训练贯穿于英语学习中,使学习者感到明确的职业指向性。

　　(2) 专业性和实用性强。在情景对话学习中,设置具体的会话情景,并在内容上与会展活动实践对接,通过情景对话的学习和训练,提高学生英语会话技巧,积累相关会展工作经验和技能;注重案例的专业性、实用性和新颖性。

　　(3) 注重能力训练。每个单元最后都科学设计、精心组织综合训练内容,注重提高英语能力和培养职业素质。

　　(4) 为便于教师教学及学生学习参考,本书配有完整、系统的教学大纲、教学计划、习题库及课件、mp3 音频文件等教辅材料。

　　本书由长春职业技术学院李世平、陈颖任主编。长春职业技术学院于海波为本书的编写做了大量的前期行业调研和资料查阅工作,长春职业技术学院张兆敏和南开大学滨海学院马宏伟负责图片遴选及文字校对等工作,在此一并致以诚挚谢意!

　　本书成稿后先后进行了十余次全面修订,但由于时间和编者水平所限,错误、疏漏之处在所难免,我们衷心希望广大英语教师和读者不吝指正,以便再版时予以修订,使本书渐臻成熟、完善。

编　者

【资源索引】

目录 Contents

Unit 1　Brief Introduction to the Exhibition and Convention Industry(会展产业简介) 1

Unit 2　Advertising(广告) 17

Unit 3　Invitation(邀请) 32

Unit 4　Choice of Venues(场馆选择) 46

Unit 5　Attending an Exhibition(参加展览) 60

Unit 6　Booth Decorating(展位装饰) 74

Unit 7　Reception at the Booth(展台接待) 88

Unit 8　Sales Presentation(销售展示) 102

Unit 9　Business Negotiation(商务谈判) 116

Unit 10　Insurance(保险) 130

Unit 11　Contract Signing(签订合同) 143

Unit 12　Handling Complaints(处理投诉) 158

Unit 13　Exhibition Dismantling(撤展) 171

Unit 14　Contacting after the Exhibition(展后联系) 184

Unit 15　Exhibition Assessment(展会评估) 197

参考文献 210

Unit 1

Brief Introduction to the Exhibition and Convention Industry
会展产业简介

Learning Objectives 学习目标

After learning this unit, you will be able to:
★ Know the history of trade shows & exhibitions.
★ Have a general understanding of the exhibition and convention industry.
★ Know how to make an introduction to exhibitions.
★ Master some useful professional words, phrases and key sentence patterns.

Background Information 背景知识

会展是会议、展览、大型活动等集体性商业或非商业活动的简称，是在一定地域空间，许多人聚集在一起形成的、定期或不定期、制度或非制度的传递和交流信息的群众性社会活动，其概念的外延包括各种类型的博览会、展览展销活动、大型会议、体育竞技运动、文化活动、节庆活动等。狭义的会展仅指展览会和会议；广义的会展是会议、展览会、节事活动和奖励旅游的统称。会议、展览会、博览会、交易会、展销会、展示会等是会展活动的基本形式，世界博览会是最典型的会展活动。

Lead-in 导入活动

【拓展视频】

Numerous companies are learning that holding a marketing event, such as conventions and exhibitions, can be a very cost-effective form of advertising in knowing their customer base. Furthermore, successful marketing events can secure new clients and sales, thus generating added revenue for the company, in attempt to advertising the company and it's products.

Exhibitions are now a very important business part in our lives and are quickly becoming the only media where buyers, sellers and products physically come together, as well as a potent force for business with the following characteristics:

◇ Highly targeted.
◇ Flexible.
◇ A two-way communication process.
◇ A neutral sales environment, for both buyers and sellers.
◇ Fast market penetration.
◇ Most cost-effective means of exploring and entering new markets.

Unit 1

会展产业简介
Brief Introduction to the Exhibition and Convention Industry

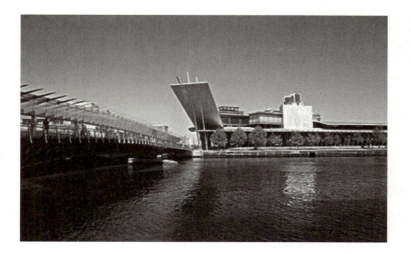

Warm-up 热身活动

Match and Discuss

Directions: Please look at the following pictures and read the descriptions of different types of events. Match each picture with the right description respectively.

1.

   A. Trade exhibitions are generally designed to meet the needs of one particular type of business, product or country. Only people involved in the field are invited to attend and the general public is rarely included.

2.

   B. A conference is a meeting with an organized agenda for delegates who have common education, communication or networking objectives.

3.

C. An incentive is a reward of recognition or a loyalty program, which is a business tool used to change behavior to improve profit, cash flow, employee engagement and customer commitment.

4.

D. Consumer exhibitions usually involve a range of products from a number of different industries on display to the general public.

Basic Reading 基础阅读

History of Trade Shows & Exhibitions

It is believed that exhibitions or trade fairs began almost 600 years before the birth of Christ. While no precise record is available, the book of Ezekiel (in the Bible) written in 588 BC, contains many references to merchants trading in a "multitude of the kinds of riches with silver, iron, tin and lead". Ezekiel also talks about the city of Tyre which used to be an important center of trade and commerce.

Today, Trade Shows & Exhibitions provide a forum for companies to display and demonstrate their products to potential buyers who have a special interest in buying these products. The compacted time frames and the focused trade show locations, are cost-effective for the exhibiting companies and convenient for the buyers.

Since the 1960s, trade shows and exhibitions are commonly used as an important part of a marketing strategy. Their relative importance is reflected in their promotional expenditures. Larger amounts of money are spent each year on trade exhibitions as compared to magazine, radio, and out-door advertising.

The primary role of trade shows, in the marketing strategy, is that of a selling medium. Depending on the type of product being exhibited, selling activities can involve booking orders or developing leads for future sales. If show regulations permit, they can even involve selling products directly at the exhibition.

Exhibitions provide a natural and nearly perfect platform for the delivery of solutions to the buyers. More and more exhibition organizers are providing learning content, demonstration theaters, and advice-giving opportunities as important features of their events. Constantly, exhibiting companies are taking full advantage of these opportunities.

Trade shows also serve as vehicles for advertising and publicity. Exhibits can be very effective three-dimensional advertisements as well as collection points for names for direct-mailing lists. They can also command the attention of the news media, which regularly cover shows in search of stories on new products and new approaches.

Participating companies can also accomplish non-promotional marketing objectives at trade shows. Market research data can be collected from show visitors. Competitors' offerings can be evaluated. And contacts can be made with potential suppliers and sales representatives.

Business-to-business trade shows are exhibitions in the areas of health care, computer products, electronics, advertising specialties, heavy equipment, agriculture, fashions, furniture and toys, focusing on goods and services within an industry or a specialized part of an industry. They are targeted to wholesalers and retailers with the intent of pushing products through a channel of distribution. Most attendees at these shows are actively looking for products and have the authority to make purchases. Consumer trade shows, like business-to-business expositions, also have an industry focus. They are different in that they target the general public, and therefore are designed to stimulate end-user demand. The kinds of products exhibited at these open shows include autos, housewares, boats, antiques and crafts.

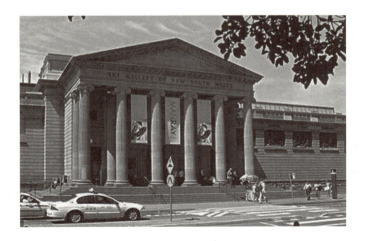

Vocabulary

precise	[prɪ'saɪs]	*adj.*	精确的
available	[ə'veɪləbl]	*adj.*	可利用的

reference	['refrəns]	n.	参考
merchant	['mɜːtʃənt]	n.	商人
multitude	['mʌltɪtjuːd]	n.	大量
frame	[freɪm]	n.	框架
expenditure	[ɪk'spendɪtʃə(r)]	n.	支出
primary	['praɪməri]	adj.	主要的；初级的
regulation	[,regju'leɪʃn]	n.	管理；规则
permit	[pə'mɪt]	v.	许可；允许
theater	['θɪətə(r)]	n.	戏院；剧场
dimensional	[daɪ'menʃənl]	adj.	<数>维的
accomplish	[ə'kʌmplɪʃ]	v.	实现
wholesaler	['həʊlseɪlə(r)]	n.	批发商
retailer	['riːteɪlə(r)]	n.	零售商
craft	[krɑːft]	n.	工艺；手艺
distribution	[,dɪstrɪ'bjuːʃn]	n.	分配；分销
authority	[ɔː'θɒrəti]	n.	权威；当局
stimulate	['stɪmjuleɪt]	v.	刺激；鼓舞
houseware	['haʊ,swɛr]	n.	家居用品
antique	[æn'tiːk]	n.	古董

Notes

1. It is believed that exhibitions or trade fairs began almost 600 years before the birth of Christ.
   据说展览或贸易展览会大概始于基督诞生前 600 年。

2. While no precise record is available, the book of Ezekiel (in the Bible) written in 588 BC, contains many references to merchants trading in a "multitude of the kinds of riches with silver, iron, tin and lead".
   虽然没有可找到的精确记录，写于公元前 588 年的《以西结书》（见《圣经》）中有很多关于商人们进行"大宗矿产如银、铁、锡、铅交易"的记载。

3. More and more exhibition organizers are providing learning content, demonstration theaters, and advice-giving opportunities as important features of their events.
   越来越多的展览组织者以提供学习内容、展演厅及建议的机会作为展览的主要特色。

4. They can also command the attention of the news media, which regularly cover shows in search of stories on new products and new approaches.
   他们也可以吸引那些定期报道展会以捕捉新产品及新方法的新闻媒体们。

5. They are targeted to wholesalers and retailers with the intent of pushing products through a

channel of distribution.

他们主要面向那些想要通过分销渠道推销产品的批发商和零售商们。

Discuss the following questions with your partner

1. Why are Trade Shows & Exhibitions perfect desirable places for a company to sell its products to potential buyers?

2. What roles do exhibitions play? Please list some of the reasons here.

3. What is a business-to-business trade show? Please give some examples.

 Situational Dialogues 情景对话

【拓展术语】

Dialogue 1

Mr. Chen contacts Mr. Fox at the Guangzhou Import and Export Commodities Fair. They are discussing the convention and exhibition industry in recent years in China.

C= Mr. Chen   F= Mr. Fox

C: Hello, Mr. Fox. I am glad to meet you here.

F: Me too. It's ages since we met last time. How have you been?

C: Everything is going well, except that I have been busy with exhibitions recently.

F: I can imagine how busy you are, with your business being very successful.

C: Yes. It is all due to various kinds of trade exhibitions and fairs.

F: You are right. I've sensed a boom these past years in the convention and exhibition industries. Does your company participate in the Guangzhou Import & Export Commodities Fair every year?

C: Yes, I don't see a good reason not to. A trade fair is one of the most effective mediums for establishing and maintaining customer relations.

F: That's right. Trade fairs involve a two-way communication process. Exhibitors can give and seek information. Most importantly, business is conducted face to face—the most persuasive form of selling, while building customer relationships.

C: That's why we never pass up a chance to participate in trade fairs in our country.

F: Does your company also promote your products by advertisements, direct mailing or a website?

C: Yes, they are very effective and most advanced in the marketplace. However, at an exhibition, buyers can see, touch and try the products for themselves. Nothing beats the impact of a live demonstration.

F: Does your company really benefit a lot from the fairs?

C: Yes, we can achieve more potential sales in a few days at a fair than we could achieve in many months using other methods of selling.

F: Yes. I can see that the China convention and exhibition industry is becoming more mature than ever before. Good luck with your future sales while you are at the exhibitions and fairs.

C: Thank you and the same to you.

Vocabulary

booming	[ˈbuːmɪŋ]	adj.	繁荣的
commodity	[kəˈmɒdəti]	n.	商品
fair	[feə(r)]	n.	展览会
effective	[ɪˈfektɪv]	adj.	有效的
medium	[ˈmiːdiəm]	n.	媒体
maintain	[meɪnˈteɪn]	v.	维持
communication	[kəˌmjuːnɪˈkeɪʃn]	n.	交流
conduct	[kənˈdʌkt]	n.	进行；实施
persuasive	[pəˈsweɪsɪv]	adj.	有说服力的
relationship	[rɪˈleɪʃnʃɪp]	n.	关系
advanced	[ədˈvɑːnst]	adj.	先进的
demonstration	[ˌdemənˈstreɪʃn]	n.	示范
mature	[məˈtʃʊə(r)]	adj.	成熟的
achieve	[əˈtʃiːv]	v.	达到；完成

Notes

1. Everything is going well.
   一切都进行得很顺利。
2. It is all due to various kinds of trade exhibitions and fairs.
   这一切都归功于各种贸易展览会。
3. I've sensed a boom these past years in the convention and exhibition industry.
   我已经感觉到这些年来会展行业的繁荣发展。
4. A trade fair is one of the most effective mediums for establishing and maintaining customer relations.
   贸易展览会是建立和维护客户关系最有效的媒介之一。
5. two-way communication 双向沟通；双向交流；双向传播

6. face to face 面对面

7. That's why we never pass up a chance to participate in trade fairs in our country.
   这就是为什么我们从不放过任何一个在本国参加交易会的机会的原因。

Dialogue 2

【拓展音频】

Tom is asking Professor Wang about the World Expo.

W=Professor Wang   T=Tom

T: Good morning, Professor Wang. May I ask you a few questions about the World Expo?

W: Sure.

T: Is the World Expo a type of commercial Expo?

W: No. It is a large-scale, global, non-commercial Expo. It aims to promote the exchange of ideas and the development of the world economy, culture, science and technology. It allows exhibitors to publicize and display their achievements and improve international relationships.

T: How far does it go back in years?

W: It has a 150-year history, since 1851 when the Great Exhibition of Industries of All Nations was held in London.

T: I heard that the Expo 2010 Shanghai was the first registered World Expo in a developing country.

W: Right. It gave the attendees a good impression, and expectation of China's future development.

T: I heard that about 200 countries and international organizations attended the World Expo 2010 Shanghai.

W: Yes, it was an unparalleled large-scale exposition.

T: When and where is the next world exposition going to be held?

W: The World Expo is divided into two types: those which are "registered" and cover a broad or general theme, and those which concentrate on a specific theme. The former is held every five years and lasts six months. And the latter usually lasts three months and is held once between the "registered" Expos. The latter one (professional exposition) will be held in South Korea in 2012 and the former one (comprehensive exposition) will be held in Milan, Italy in 2015.

T: Thanks for your professional explanation, Professor Wang.

W: You're welcome.

Vocabulary

exposition	[ˌekspəˈzɪʃn]	n.	博览会
scale	[skeɪl]	n.	规模
commercial	[kəˈmɜːʃl]	adj.	商业的
exchange	[ɪksˈtʃeɪndʒ]	n.	交换
publicize	[ˈpʌblɪsaɪz]	v.	宣传
achievement	[əˈtʃiːvmənt]	n.	成就
registered	[ˈredʒɪstəd]	adj.	注册的
expectation	[ˌekspekˈteɪʃn]	n.	期待
unparalleled	[ʌnˈpærəleld]	adj.	无比的
recognize	[ˈrekəgnaɪz]	v.	识别

Notes

1. May I ask you a few questions about the World Expo?
   我可以问你几个关于世界博览会的问题吗?

2. Is the World Expo a type of commercial Expo?
   世界博览会是商业博览会吗?

3. It is a large-scale, global, and non-commercial Expo.
   它是大规模的、全球性的非商业性博览会。

4. It aims to promote the exchange of ideas and the development of the world economy, culture, science and technology.
   它旨在促进思想交流及世界经济、文化、科学和技术的发展。

5. The World Expo is divided into two types.
   世界博览会分为两种类型。

6. It was an unparalleled large-scale exposition.
   这是一个无与伦比的大型博览会。

Useful Sentences 常用口语

【拓展音频】

1. I see that the MICE industry in China is becoming more mature than ever before.
   我能够看到中国的会展业正变得比以往任何时候都更加成熟。

2. What would be a nice location for our Kitchen wares?
   我们要举办的厨房用品展览选址在哪里比较合适呢?

3. This location is very convenient for attendees, visitors, and freight delivery.
   对于参展人员、参观者和货运来说,这个位置都非常便利。

4. It caters to a variety of needs and interests for participants.
   它满足了参加者的各种需求和偏好。
5. We provide our customers with a series of high-quality services.
   我们为客户提供了一系列优质服务。
6. Selecting a suitable venue is the common desire of organizers, contractors and participants.
   挑选合适的场馆是组织者、承办者和参与者三方的共同愿望。
7. Selecting the correct venue for your trade show involves many important considerations.
   要选择适合你的展览场馆，应进行多方面的考虑。
8. Trade fairs involve a two-way communication process.
   商品交易会涉及一个双向交流沟通的过程。
9. That's why we never pass up any chance to participate in trade shows in our country.
   这就是为什么我们从来没有放弃在本国参加贸易展览会的机会的原因。
10. Nothing beats the impact of a live show.
    现场展示所产生的影响是其他任何方式都比不了的。
11. World Expositions provide exhibitors the opportunity to advertise and display their achievements and improve international relationships.
    世界博览会给参展方提供机会来宣传展示其成就和改善国际关系。
12. A trade fair is one of the most effective mediums for establishing and maintaining customer relations.
    贸易展览会是建立和维护客户关系的最有效的媒介之一。

 Further Reading 拓展阅读

Fairs, Expositions and Exhibitions

The roots of the phenomenon "Fairs, Expositions and Exhibitions" can be traced back to its language origin.

"Fair" comes from Latin "feria", meaning "holiday" as well as "market fair". This in turn corresponds to the Latin "feriae", which cames to mean a religious festival. During the 12th century, as the importance of trade meetings increased, fairs were held close to churches, so that the concept of religious festival and market fair is combined in a common language.

The word "exhibition" was mentioned as early as 1649. It is a derivative of the Latin word "expositio", meaning "displaying" or "putting on a show". Exhibitions are not just collections of interesting objects brought together at a certain place and time. They are human activities, and human enterprises, undertaken for definite reasons in order to achieve certain specified results. They are a form of human exchange, whereby the promoters and exhibitors communicate with the visitors. Their results can only be told in terms of further human thoughts and activities.

The word "exposition" goes back to the same origin as "exhibition". Expositions, rooted in old French, tended to be very similar to their English cousins, and exhibitions. Expositions were held in facilities built specifically for them. They were organized by either government departments or groups of entrepreneurs with government assistance for the express purpose of promoting trade. Manufacturers were invited to show their goods. In colloquial speech the concepts are used similarly. However, there are some interesting conceptual developments which show the variability of today's exhibition industry.

Fair

The Middle English word "feire", which means a gathering of people held at regular intervals for the barter or sales of goods, is the one from which the present definition, i.e. a periodic gathering for sales of goods, often with shows or entertainment, at a place and time fixed by custom, is taken.

Expositions and Exhibitions

Expositions and exhibitions have always been combined with the display of goods and products. Exhibitions differed from fairs in four major ways.

Firstly, exhibitions were usually one-time events. They did not enjoy a recurring life cycle. However, fairs ran for a short period of time, many exhibitions ran for months, and some for a year or longer.

Secondly, exhibitions were housed in permanent facilities built specifically for them. Starting in the 18th century, the practice of building a facility for the express purpose of housing an exhibition was the precursor of the exposition/convention industry.

Thirdly, although fairs were held regularly, they were not highly-organized events. Over time, religious and later civic leaders did take the control of the grounds where fairs were held (usually public lands). Exhibitions, on the other hand, were highly-organized events. They were initially created by government departments or committees for the purpose of promoting trade.

Finally, exhibitions differed from fairs in the very way in which business was conducted. Goods were bought and sold at fairs. At exhibitions, commercial activity or sales of the displayed goods was not usually involved. However, inherence in displaying the goods was the hope of stimulating future sales. Today this is how most exhibitions still operate.

Unit 1

会展产业简介
Brief Introduction to the Exhibition and Convention Industry

Vocabulary

phenomenon	[fəˈnɒmɪnən]	n.	现象
correspond	[ˌkɒrəˈspɒnd]	v.	符合；一致
derivative	[dɪˈrɪvətɪv]	n.	衍生物
cousin	[ˈkʌzn]	n.	堂兄弟姐妹
variability	[ˌveəriəˈbɪləti]	n.	变化性
entrepreneur	[ˌɒntrəprəˈnɜː(r)]	n.	企业家
colloquial	[kəˈləʊkwiəl]	adj.	通俗的
conceptual	[kənˈseptʃuəl]	adj.	概念上的
facility	[fəˈsɪləti]	n.	设施
interval	[ˈɪntəvl]	n.	间隔
barter	[ˈbɑːtə(r)]	n.	易货贸易
recur	[rɪˈkɜː(r)]	v.	重现
permanent	[ˈpɜːmənənt]	adj.	永久的
precursor	[priˈkɜːsə(r)]	n.	先驱
initially	[ɪˈnɪʃəli]	adv.	最初
inherent	[ɪnˈherənt]	adj.	固有的
stimulate	[ˈstɪmjuleɪt]	v.	刺激；鼓舞

Notes

1. The roots of the phenomenon "Fairs, Expositions and Exhibitions" can be traced back to its language origin.
   "展览会、博览会和展览"这种现象的根源可以追溯到其语言的起源。
2. This in turn corresponds to the Latin "feriae", which comes to mean a religious festival.
   这个词与拉丁语"feriae"相对应，其含义是一种宗教节日。
3. Expositions were held in facilities built specifically for them.
   当时的展会在专门建造的场馆内举行。
4. However, there are some interesting conceptual developments which show the variability of today's exhibition industry.
   然而，一些有趣的概念上的变化体现了今天会展业的变化。
5. Secondly, exhibitions were housed in permanent facilities built specifically for them.
   其次，展览被置于专为其建造的永久性设施中。
6. Over time, religious and later civic leaders did take the control of the grounds where fairs were held (usually public lands).
   随着时间的推移，宗教领袖和后来的市民领袖也曾控制了用来举办集市的场地（通常是公共场地）。
7. However, inherence in displaying the goods was the hope of stimulating future sales.
   然而，展示商品的本意是希望促进未来的销售。

Answer the following questions.

1. What is the difference among Fairs, Expositions and Exhibitions?
2. What is the main difference between Exhibitions and Fairs?

Decide whether the following statements are True or False based on the above passage.

1. Both "Fair" and "Exhibition" come from the Latin language. (　)
2. Expositions were held for the purpose of promoting religious activities. (　)
3. Today's Fairs are also held at regular intervals for the barter or sales of goods. (　)
4. Exhibitions were usually one-time events while Fairs were recurring ones. (　)
5. It is unnecessary to hold exhibitions in permanent facilities built specifically for them. (　)
6. Fairs and Exhibitions were highly organized by government departments or committees. (　)

Unit 1

会展产业简介
Brief Introduction to the Exhibition and Convention Industry

Exercises

1. Match the words on the left with their proper meaning on the right.

(1) precise   a. the act of grasping
(2) merchant   b. happen or occur again
(3) multitude   c. keep in a certain state, position or activity
(4) frame   d. a state of economic prosperity
(5) permit   e. the power or right to give orders
(6) authority   f. consent to
(7) boom   g. a structure supporting something
(8) maintain   h. a large gathering of people
(9) recur   i. a businessperson engaged in retail trade
(10) hold   j. sharply exact

2. Read the following statements, and fill in the blank spaces with the appropriate words contained in the word box.

| public   product   price   buyers   globe   things |

(1) When you consider the history of trade shows and exhibiting in general, you start thinking about how long people have been selling _____ to one another.

(2) It's a fundamental principle of business survival that has prevailed throughout the history and around the _____.

(3) Historically, trade shows likely started with people simply displaying their wares in _____ places.

(4) They took time to talk individually with potential _____ about what they have to offer.

(5) Then, they negotiated a purchase _____ (or bartered goods or services) until a mutual agreement was met.

(6) At one time, exhibiting was likely one of the only ways to "market" your _____, and perhaps served as a necessary survival tactic to provide for their families.

3. Translate the following sentences into English.

(1) 我们为客户提供了高质量的产品和服务。
(2) 选择合适的场馆是组织者、承办者和参与者三方的共同愿望。
(3) 现场展示所产生的影响是其他任何营销方式都无法企及的。
(4) 展览会是建立和维护客户关系的最有效的媒介之一。

4. Role play.

Make up a dialogue based on the following situation.

You work as a receptionist at the Chengdu Kitchenware Company Limited. A client is interested in your Kitchen-wares. How will you introduce your products to him.

　　* If you use illustrations, make sure they're clear and uncomplicated.

　　* If you use translations, get each language version "reality check" by a native speaker.

　　Finally, you need to test the instructions on people who are genuinely typical of the target audience.

 Practical Training Project 实训项目

　　Perform research on the Internet, concerning an international exhibition center that is of interest to your company. Prepare a 10-minute presentation for introducing the venue and recommending why your company should choose this venue.

Unit 2

Advertising

广 告

Learning Objectives 学习目标

After learning this unit, you will be able to:
★ Understand exhibition advertising methods.
★ Identify the characteristics of each method of advertising.
★ Promote exhibitions through various forms of communication.
★ Learn useful words and expressions concerning this topic.

Background Information 背景知识

广告是为了某种特定的需要,通过一定形式的媒体,公开而广泛地向公众传递信息的宣传手段。要想使广告达到最佳效果,媒体的选择至关重要。

会展经常用的广告媒体有:印刷媒体、广播影视、户外媒体、直复媒体、互联网媒体、包装媒体、交通媒体等。

Lead-in 导入活动

【拓展视频】

Advertising is the lucrative way of bringing forth the unique selling proportion (USP) of a product. A company can advertise through a number of mediums, including newspapers, magazines, display booths, TV, radio, billboards, Internet, etc.

Exhibition advertising is a blend of "exhibition" and "advertising", while providing the exhibition advertiser with a double benefit. It helps a company to highlight itself, as well as showcase its products and services to a target audience, and as a result grow their business.

Unit 2 广告 Advertising

Warm-up 热身活动

Match and Discuss

Directions: Please look at the following pictures and read the descriptions of selected exhibition tools. Match each picture with the right description respectively.

1.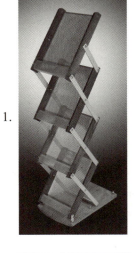

    A. **Product Name:**
    Banner Stand
    Description: Banner stand with three feet. Double-sided use. Foldaway feet.

2.

    B. **Product Name:**
    Brochure Stand, Brochure Holder
    Description: Punched steel with wood edge and bottom.
    It can hold all kinds of brochures.
    Silk-screen processing available.

3.

    C. **Product Name:**
    Light Box, Outdoor Stand, Flag Banners
    Description: For outdoor use, Flag stand with tank.
    Features: (1) Wind resistant, with a stable and stylish design. (2) Light weight.

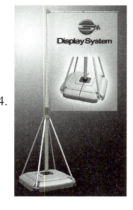

4.

Product Name:

D.　Promotion Stand

Model No.: CC-1.

Trade Show Advertising Ideas

Trade show is a great way to get your product or service in front of prospective customers, but how can you set yourself apart from your competitions, and attract new business? In order to build a crowd around your table, prepare before the show by developing a comprehensive plan that will attract attention. If you have some free goodies for people and an outgoing attitude, it will be much easier to earn orders and build a contact sheet that will bring you lots of future sales.

※ **Before the Show**

　　Make a detailed plan about what you will do during the show. Jon Edelman from TradeShowMarketing.com says you should figure out your niche within the scope of the rest of the attendees. He lists four bullet points, by which you should consider these rivals: target market (who they serve), pricing (yours in comparison with theirs), promotion (how and where they advertise) and strengths and weaknesses (how much of a threat they are to your business). After doing this, you will be able to address questions prospective customers will have, and can let people know why they should form a relationship with you. Provide freebies, branded with your contact information that you can give away during the show. Companies such as Promopeddler.com can customize calendars, candy and more. They also advise you to send an e-mail to attendees a week prior to the event, letting them know they should visit your booth for a free giveaway.

※ **At the Show**

　　Create some excitement by having employees walk around the show, and distributing flyers for your business. Have them wear clothes that feature your company's logo. It's also important to brief the workers so they know about your products or services in case they get questions. You should produce as much of a "show" as is allowed by the people running the event (Check the guidelines you received when you rented your event space). Be outgoing, walk around to speak with people, and encourage them to visit your booth. Quite often, if you get just a few people to come to your booth, and watch your presentation, others will stop to see what all the excitement is about.

※ **After the Show**

Maintain a mailing list, and get as many people as possible to sign up. This gives you the opportunity to contact them via e-mail or snail mail in the coming weeks. Further, this should be done within a couple weeks after the event, so the contact hasn't had time to forget about you, and make sure you are still fresh in his or her mind.

Vocabulary

prospective	[prəˈspektɪv]	adj.	未来的
outgoing	[ˈaʊtgəʊɪŋ]	adj.	乐于助人的
niche	[niːʃ]	n.	利基；合适的职业
scope	[skəʊp]	n.	范围
bullet	[ˈbʊlɪt]	n.	子弹
rival	[ˈraɪvl]	n.	对手
comparison	[kəmˈpærɪsn]	n.	比较
threat	[θret]	n.	威胁
customize	[ˈkʌstəmaɪz]	v.	定制；定做
calendar	[ˈkælɪndə(r)]	n.	日历
distributing	[dɪˈstrɪbjuːtɪŋ]	adj.	分配的
via	[ˈvaɪə]	prep.	通过

Notes

1. Trade show is a great way to get your product or service in front of prospective customers, but how can you set yourself apart from your competitions, and attract new business?
   展销会是一种将你的产品或服务呈现在你的潜在客户面前的极好方式,但是如何才能使你在竞争中独树一帜,发展新的业务呢?

2. Jon Edelman from TradeShowMarketing.com says you should figure out your niche within the scope of the rest of the attendees.
   来自会展营销公司的乔恩·爱德曼先生指出,你要清楚自己在参展者中的位置。

3. After doing this, you will be able to address questions prospective customers will have, and can let people know why they should form a relationship with you.
   完成这项工作后,你就能够应对未来客户可能提出的问题,而且让客户知道为什么他们应该与你建立业务关系。

4. Companies such as Promopeddler.com can customize calendars, candy and more.
   像 Promopeddler 这样的公司能够定制日历、糖果等。

5. It's also important to brief the workers, so they know about your products or services in case they get questions.
   为工作人员做简单介绍也是很重要的。这样,他们就能够了解你们的产品和服务,而不会有疑问。

6. You should produce as much of a "show" as is allowed by the people running the event.
   你应该在展会管理人员允许的范围内尽可能创造"秀场"效果。

Discuss the following question with your partner.

What are the best ways to attract an attendee's attention during the trade show?

Situational Dialogues 情景对话

Dialogue 1

【拓展术语】

In the following dialogue, Mr. Black is representing his company and will discuss with Ms. Liu, the manager of the advertising department at an exhibition and conference center, concerning the arrangement of advertisements prior to his company attending an exhibition.

Unit 2 广告 Advertising

B=Mr. Black   L=Ms. Liu

B: Good morning! Nice to meet you!

L: Good morning! It's my pleasure to meet you too.

B: Our company will participate in this exhibition, so would you please give me a brief introduction of your advertising arrangements?

L: Sure. Which one would you be interested in, indoor advertising or outdoor advertising?

B: Outdoor advertising.

L: For outdoor advertisements, we will prepare a large balloon, colored flags, billboards, banners, etc. But some outdoor advertisement will be an additional charge.

B: I see. Do you have any advertisements on the Internet?

L: Yes, we have Internet advertising on our own website.

B: How many hits do you have on your website each month?

L: Over 50 000 hits each month.

B: That's good. Can our company have advertisements on your website?

L: You can buy a banner advertisements or a link to your own website.

B: Great! We will discuss about this later. Then what kind of indoor advertisement do you have?

L: For indoor advertisements, we will prepare some banners, posters, billboards, etc. You can choose your favorite form of advertising in accordance with your budget.

B: Thank you. I will think about these options.

L: You can visit our website to get more specific information about our advertisement capabilities. You can find our website address in this brochure.

B: Thank you.

L: You are welcome.

Vocabulary

balloon	[bəˈluːn]	n.	气球
billboard	[ˈbɪlbɔːd]	n.	广告牌
banner	[ˈbænə(r)]	n.	横幅
charge	[tʃɑːdʒ]	n.	费用
hit	[hɪt]	n.	点击量
option	[ˈɒpʃn]	n.	选择
poster	[ˈpəʊstə(r)]	n.	海报；广告
accordance	[əˈkɔːdns]	n.	一致
budget	[ˈbʌdʒɪt]	n.	预算

Notes

1. Would you please give me a brief introduction of your advertising arrangements?
   你能否向我简单介绍一下你的广告计划？

2. indoor advertising 室内广告；outdoor advertising 户外广告
   For example: Which one would you be interested in, indoor advertising or outdoor advertising?
   例如：你想先了解哪方面呢，室内广告还是户外广告？

3. Some outdoor advertisements will be an additional charge.
   一些户外推广项目会另外收费。

4. How many hits do you have on your website each month?
   你们网站每个月有多少点击量？

5. Over 50 000 hits each month.
   每月超过 5 万次的点击量。

6. in accordance with 与……一致；依照
   For example: You can choose your favorite form of advertising in accordance with your budget.
   例如：你可以根据预算选择你喜欢的广告形式。

Dialogue 2

【拓展音频】

S=staff　　C=customer

S: Good morning, Changchun International Conference and Exhibition Center Advertising Department, how may I help you?

C: Yes. This is Mr. Black from Northern Fashion Company. I'd like to know something about the trade show advertising in your center.

S: Sure. Our department specializes in assisting companies in advertising the products. We can help you reach a target audience by placing backlit signs, banners or posters at various locations in the exhibition space.

C: I see. How about per show advertising?

S: For per show advertising, locations are available at our lobby entrance. We will place your business name, and list your products and your booth number at a premier location. Your company can get the exposure of all the attendees.

C: That's very good. Could you please tell me something about your Internet advertising?

S: Sure. Thousands of people use our website for show information. We receive more than 30 000 hits on our website each month.

Unit 2
广告 Advertising

C: That's a good exposure, and a good choice for advertisements. Can you provide us with some further information about your pricing? We'd like to visit your website firstly, and then consider placing some advertisements online. For your reference, our fax number is 632333, and please send everything to my attention, Mr. Black.

Vocabulary

specialize	[ˈspeʃəlaɪz]	v.	专门从事
assist	[əˈsɪst]	v.	帮助
various	[ˈveəriəs]	adj.	各种各样的
location	[ləʊˈkeɪʃn]	n.	位置
available	[əˈveɪləbl]	adj.	可利用的
lobby	[ˈlɒbi]	n.	大厅；休息室
entrance	[ˈentrəns]	n.	入口
premier	[ˈpremiə(r)]	adj.	第一的；最初的
exposure	[ɪkˈspəʊʒə(r)]	n.	亮相

Notes

1. specialize in 专门经营；擅长

   For example: Our department specializes in assisting companies in advertising the products.
   例如：我们部门专门帮助公司推广产品

2. target audience 目标客户

   For example: We can help you reach a target audience by placing backlit signs, banners or posters at various locations in the exhibition space.
   例如：我们通过在展位的不同位置放置发光的标识牌、横幅或者海报来帮你吸引目标客户群。

3. How about per show advertising?
   单次展览广告是怎样的？

4. For per show advertising, locations are available at our lobby entrance.
   单次展览广告，位置在我们大厅入口处。

5. provide with 供给；为……装备上

   For example: Can you provide us with some more information about your pricing?
   例如：可否提供有关报价的信息？

【拓展音频】

Useful Sentences 常用口语

1. Would you please give me a brief introduction of your advertising arrangements?
   你能否向我简单介绍一下你的广告计划？

2. Which one would you be interested in, indoor advertising or outdoor advertising?
   你想先了解哪方面呢，室内广告还是户外广告？

3. For outdoor advertisement, we will prepare a large balloon, colored flags, billboards, banners, etc.
   在户外推广时，我们会准备一只大气球、一些彩旗、展板、横幅等。

4. Some outdoor advertisements will be an additional charge.
   但是一些户外推广项目会另外收费。

5. For indoor advertisements, we will prepare some banners, posters, billboards, etc.
   在室内推广时，我们会准备一些横幅、海报、展板等。

6. You can choose your favorite form of advertising in accordance with your budget.
   你可以根据预算选择喜欢的广告形式。

7. Do you have both per show advertising and year-round advertising?
   你们是否有单次展览广告和全年广告？

8. Locations are available at our lobby entrance.
   具体位置在我们大厅入口处。

9. How many hits do you have on your website each month?
   你们的网站每个月有多少点击率？

10. You can expose your business by purchasing a banner advertising or a link to your website.
    你可以通过购买一个横幅广告或者你们的网站的链接来增加贵公司的知名度。

11. Could you please tell me something about your Internet advertising?
    可以说说你们的网络广告吗？

12. That's a good exposure, and a good choice for ads.
    高曝光率是做广告的好选择。

Further Reading 拓展阅读

How Can Trade Show Organizers Promote Trade Shows to Attract Buyers and Sellers?

Trade show organizers must utilize all the marketing strategies needed to make the show a success. This article discusses some highly effective strategies to ensure that the industry-related traders find out the upcoming show ahead of time.

Trade show organizers arrange trade shows to facilitate the process of promoting products and services for B2B (Business to Business) organizations. Trade shows have now become a powerful tool for B2B companies to give an instant exposure to their products.

B2B companies have a platform in the form of trade shows to market their products, but what should trade show organizers do to promote their shows?

Fierce competition among trade show organizers is now increasing. Not only do they face challenges from their direct competitors, but they also compete against other organizations, such as advertising agencies and consultants who want a share of corporate marketing budgets as well. Therefore, it is essential to promote the shows in an influential manner.

Here are the strategies you can apply, as a trade show organizer to promote your trade shows and attract buyers and sellers from relevant industries around the world.

1. The Media

Put the power of the media to work for you. Whether newspapers, magazines, radio or TV, you will be able to put the message across and create awareness of your shows. Tailor your message according to the needs of your target audience. Providing powerful industry-related stats will immensely enhance the appeal of your show.

2. Press Release

Press release is another extremely powerful tool for creating awareness of something new or improved. Write a press release, keep focus on the proper format, or else, otherwise it will be rejected by the reporter. If you are unaware of the particulars involved in writing, get it written by a professional writer. Once done, submit it to a reporter to review it, and to publish it.

3. Trade Directories

There are dozens of trade directories online that publish information about upcoming trade shows, cities they will be conducted in, and industries they will cover. Submitting information about your upcoming show to such directories is a highly productive way of marketing your show in a very short span of time.

4. Industry-Related Publications

Promote your shows in trade or industry-related publications. As each show covers a specific category, find publications that cover the same category as your show and market your shows there. Buyers and sellers look for information related to trade show in such publications and, hence, this will enable you to convey the message to the most target audience.

5. Industry-Related Websites

Industry-related websites play a significant role in promoting your shows. They are as effective as offline industry-related publications. Look for vertical portals online as this is where you will find your target market. Promote your trade shows on vertical portals and you will end up attracting an enormous amount of interested and qualified industry-related traders.

6. B2B Websites

You will undoubtedly find millions of buyers and suppliers on B2B websites. Even though your show will be organized around a closely defined category, you can be sure to find thousands of relevant traders on B2B portals. Some B2B portals have a dedicated section for trade shows. For example, TradeKey.com, world's leading B2B platform, has a complete section http://tradeshow.tradekey.com the for trade show organizers where they can post and promote their shows.

Final Words

In today's competitive world, if you want to stay ahead of your competitors, you must promote your services or products in a highly effective manner. Make sure you utilize as many means as possible to promote your trade shows, both locally and globally.

Vocabulary

utilize	['juːtəlaɪz]	v.	利用
facilitate	[fə'sɪlɪteɪt]	v.	促进
fierce	[fɪəs]	adj.	猛烈的
consultant	[kən'sʌltənt]	n.	咨询者
influential	[ˌɪnflu'enʃl]	adj.	有影响的
tailor	['teɪlə(r)]	v.	剪裁；使合适
immensely	[ɪ'mensli]	adv.	极大地
reject	[rɪ'dʒekt]	v.	拒绝；丢弃
convey	[kən'veɪ]	v.	传达；运输
significant	[sɪg'nɪfɪkənt]	adj.	有意义的
vertical	['vɜːtɪkl]	adj.	垂直的
portal	['pɔːtl]	n.	门户网站；入口
dedicate	['dedɪkeɪt]	v.	致力；献身

Unit 2
广 告
Advertising

Notes

1. Put the power of the media to work for you.
   借助媒体的力量为您服务。
2. Providing powerful industry-related stats will immensely enhance the appeal of your show.
   提供强大的与行业相关的统计数据将极大地提高展览的吸引力。
3. Write a press release, keep focus on the proper format, or else, otherwise it will be rejected by the reporter.
   写一份新闻稿，注意格式要正确，否则它将被记者拒绝。
4. Promote your shows in trade or industry-related publications.
   在与贸易或行业相关的出版物中宣传您的展会。
5. As each show covers a specific category, find publications that cover the same category as your show and market your shows there.
   由于一个展览有一个门类，找到覆盖同一门类的出版物，为展览做市场宣传。
6. Promote your trade shows on vertical portals and you will end up attracting an enormous amount of interested and qualified industry-related traders.
   通过垂直门户网站推广您的展览会，您最终会吸引到大量感兴趣的和有资质的与产业相关的贸易商。

Answer the following questions.

1. What is a B2B trade show? Give a brief explanation.
2. What must trade show organizers do to promote their shows?

Decide whether the following statements are True or False based on the above passage.

1. Trade show organizers arrange trade shows to help promote products and services for sellers. (   )
2. Trade show organizers only have to compete with advertising companies in the markets. (   )
3. A trade show organizer can make a show known to the target audience by advertising with the media, or writing a report of your show and having it published. (   )
4. It is time-effective to promote your show on trade directories. (   )
5. Advertising trade shows on industry-related websites is a great way to bring in all kinds of traders. (   )

6. Some B2B portals have a dedicated section for trade shows.　　　　　(   )

Exercises

1. Match the words on the left with their proper meaning on the right.

(1) crowd　　　　　a. a name given to a product or service

(2) contact　　　　b. a reference point to shoot at

(3) bullet　　　　　c. a large number of people considered together

(4) rival　　　　　d. a projectile that is fired from a gun

(5) target　　　　　e. close interaction

(6) brand　　　　　f. the contestant you hope to defeat

(7) advise　　　　　g. the act of contacting one thing with another

(8) logo　　　　　　h. keep in a certain state, position or activity

(9) maintain　　　　i. a company emblem or device

(10) hit　　　　　　j. give advice to

2. Read the following statements and fill in the blank spaces with the appropriate words enclosed in the word box.

| products | public | displaying | as | way | mediums |

(1) Advertising may be defined _____ paid form of the public promotion of a product, service, company or an idea.

(2) Advertising is the lucrative _____ of bringing forth the unique selling proportion (USP) of a product.

(3) A company can advertise through a number of _____ like newspapers, magazines, display stalls, TV, radio, bill boards, Internet, etc.

(4) Exhibition is the art of _____ products and services for public viewing.

(5) The purpose of exhibiting may also vary. It may just be for the generation of business or simply for _____ viewing.

(6) Such exhibitions prove profitable for companies, who want to display their _____ to a vast number of prospective customers in a short span of time, thus saving time and money.

3. Translate the following sentences into English.

(1) 请将你的广告计划简单地给我做个介绍。

(2) 一些户外推广项目会另外收费。

(3) 我们公司网站每个月的点击率都很高。

(4) 公交车与地铁上的广告都是不错的选择。

4. Role play.

Work in pairs or more. Try to do a short play according to the following instruction.

Suppose you are an exhibitor. Immediately before the exhibition started, you found something was wrong with the design of your banners. Talk to your partner, and decide who from the exhibition company can solve this problem.

Practical Training Project 实训项目

Perform research on the Internet, concerning a trade show that is of interest to your company. Prepare an 8-minute presentation introducing the event and recommending why your company should exhibit at this event.

Unit 3

Invitation
邀　请

Unit 3 邀请 Invitation

Learning Objectives 学习目标

After learning this unit, you will be able to:

★ Know the importance of inviting people to your show.

★ Have a general understanding of how to invite people to your show.

★ Know how to ask for information about the show, provide attendance information, and personally invite exhibitors.

★ Grasp some words, expressions, key sentence patterns and typical sentences on this topic.

Background Information 背景知识

招展与招商是会展行业术语。招展是承办单位招徕参展企业来参展，从而实现从主办单位到参展企业的价值传递的过程。招商是承办单位招徕专业观众来参观展览的过程。随着会展业竞争的加剧，招展与招商已经成为展会成功举办的核心要素。

Lead-in 导入活动

An exhibition invitation is a key step of exhibition marketing, and can guarantee a successful exhibition. Prior to an exhibition, various types of communication mediums are used, such as newspapers, telephone contact, fax, E-mail, website, mail, invitation, and possibly a personal contact to invite relevant organizations to be exhibitors or sponsors.

【拓展视频】

If you want to have an effective invitation, you should follow the processes below.

◇ Determine your potential customers.

◇ Send invitations.

◇ Analyze delivery results.

◇ Telemarketing (telephone calls, and reminders before the exhibition date).

◇ Personal VIP invitations (market categorization by CRM methods).

Warm-up 热身活动

Match and Discuss

Match the pictures in the left column with the corresponding terms in the right column and discuss with your partner to see how much you understand about the services provided.

1.    A. exhibition consulting

2.    B. trade show advertising

3.    C. trade show on-line service

Unit 3
邀　请
Invitation

4. 　　　　　　　　D. trade show invitation

Basic Reading 基础阅读

Memory Jolt—Reminding Your Clients

Invite your customers to the trade show, tell them that you will be launching new products, and then give them a reason to visit the show to buy your products. Recent research has shown that 83% of the most successful companies that attend trade shows (in terms of business generated and positive leads) would endeavor to send e-mails to their prospects and customers before the show.

If every exhibitor invites 10 of their clients to the show, the visitors' attendance would be increased by 1 000 people. If you invite 50 of your clients to the show, the visitors' attendance would be increased by 5 000 people. That's a lot more potential business.

Some exhibitors have also found that by alerting their potential customer base before the show will create more business. It acts as a memory jolt. Otherwise, out of sight, out of mind! Writing to your customers prior to the show is an excuse for you to contact them and renew their interest in the show.

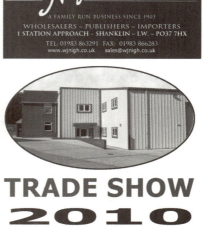

Vocabulary

jolt	[dʒəʊlt]	v.	使颠簸；使摇动
remind	[rɪ'maɪnd]	v.	提醒；使想起
launch	[lɔːntʃ]	v.	发动；开始
research	[rɪ'sɜːtʃ]	n.	研究；调查
endeavor	[ɪn'dɛvə]	v.	努力；尽力
prospect	['prɒspekt]	n.	前途；预期
potential	[pə'tenʃl]	adj.	潜在的
prior	['praɪə(r)]	adv.	在前；居先
excuse	[ɪk'skjuːs]	n.	借口；理由

Notes

1. Recent research has shown that 83% of the most successful companies that attend trade shows (in terms of business generated and positive leads) would endeavor to send e-mails to their prospects and customers before the show.

   最近的研究表明，83%参加贸易展会最有成效的公司(根据生成的业务和实际的商机)，都尽量在举办展会之前就将邮件发送给他们的客户及潜在客户。

2. That's a lot more potential business.

   这是一个更大的潜在商机。

3. Otherwise, out of sight, out of mind!

   否则，眼不见，心不烦。

4. Writing to your customers prior to the show is an excuse for you to contact them and renew their interest in the show.

   展会前写邮件给你的客户是一个联系客户并且重新引起他们对展会兴趣的很好理由。

Discuss the following questions with your partner.

1. Why is it important for an exhibitor to write invitation letters to his prospects and customers before the show?

2. What benefits can pre-show invitations bring to the exhibitors?

Unit 3

邀　　请
Invitation

【拓展术语】

Situational Dialogues 情景对话

Dialogue 1

Mr. Smith, a senior manager of sales from Datang International exhibition Co., Ltd, is communicating with Mrs. Zhang Hua by phone, who is the head of an auto parts service company in Singapore, for China International Auto Parts Expo.

S=Mr. Smith　　　Z=Mrs. Zhang Hua

S: Good morning. This is Mr. Smith speaking, from Datang International exhibition Co., Ltd. May I speak to Mrs. Zhang Hua, please?

Z: Good morning. This is Zhang Hua speaking. Mr. Smith, what can I do for you?

S: I'm pleased to welcome your company to China International Auto Parts Exposition in Beijing, China. The show will be held on Oct. 26th, 2012 to Oct. 28th, 2012.

Z: Thank you very much. But our main office has relocated this past month to Thailand, and I'm a new manager with the company. So I have no idea concerning this exhibition. May I please have more information about the Exposition?

S: Sure. China International Auto Parts Expo (CIAPE) is an elite international auto parts exhibition focusing on the global OE market, aftermarket and car accessories market. It serves as a platform for commercialization of new products, technologies and materials, and establishment of brand images.

Z: Good. But to be frank, our company is offered so many invitations to different auto parts exhibitions from different countries and regions every year. And we can only attend those that we believe would be of benefit to us.

S: Good point. I understand.

Z: Fine. I'm just wondering how you guarantee the quality of potential buyers.

S: Good question! Let me assure you that we take a sincere effort to invite buyers with strong competitiveness through various channels to participate in the exhibition; meanwhile, we keep maintaining participation conditions and invitation procedures to guarantee the quality of buyers, so that you will no doubt enjoy the great benefits at our show.

Z: It sounds very promising.

S: Are you available this afternoon? I can give you our official invitations and the exhibition specification. You will then have all of the information in order to make your decision to attend the Exposition.

Z: How kind of you! Yes, I'm free this afternoon.

S: Great. Could I meet you at 5:00 this afternoon?

37

Z: No problem.

S: Thank you for your time. See you this afternoon at your office.

Vocabulary

Thailand	['taɪlænd]	n.	泰国
elite	[eɪ'liːt]	n.	精英；精华
accessory	[ək'sesəri]	n.	配件
platform	['plætfɔːm]	n.	平台
commercialization	[kə,mɜːʃəlaɪ'zeɪʃ(ə)n]	n.	商品化
establishment	[ɪ'stæblɪʃmənt]	n.	确立
region	['riːdʒən]	n.	地区；范围
various	['veərɪəs]	adj.	各种各样的
channel	['tʃænl]	n.	通道；频道
specification	[,spesɪfɪ'keɪʃn]	n.	说明书

Notes

1. China International Auto Parts Expo (CIAPE) is an elite international auto parts exhibition.
   中国国际汽车零部件博览会是国际上汽车零部件展览会中的翘楚。

2. Focused on the global OE market, aftermarket and car accessories market.
   关注全球原始设备市场、售后市场和汽车配件市场。

3. It serves as a platform for commercialization of new products, technologies and materials, and establishment of brand images.
   它作为一个平台，服务于新产品、新技术、新材料的商业化及品牌形象的树立。

4. I'm just wondering how you guarantee the quality of potential buyers.
   我只是想知道你们如何保证潜在买家的质量。

5. Are you available this afternoon?
   您今天下午有空吗？

6. How kind of you!
   你真好啊！

【拓展音频】

Dialogue 2

At 5:00 p.m, Mr. Smith arrives at Mrs. Zhang Hua's office with the official invitation and the exhibition specification. The following is their dialogue.

S=Mr. Smith   Z=Mrs. Zhang Hua

Unit 3
邀请 Invitation

S: Nice to see you again, Mrs. Zhang Hua.

Z: Nice to see you too, Mr. Smith.

S: As promised, here is the official invitation and the exhibition specification.

Z: Thank you. I've read about the exhibition, but I'd like to know more about it.

S: Sure. I'd be very happy to give you any further information you need.

Z: Firstly, how about your media cooperation?

S: Our official media partners are leading of publications international trade show industry. They are committed to fully supporting the event by dedicating sections of their news updating pages, and special features pertaining to our event.

Z: It would be suitable for us if we were offered free advertising opportunities.

S: Actually, during the exhibition, we will hold press conferences and visual illustrations to fully display the participant's new auto parts products.

Z: Oh, excellent! I wonder if you would be able to do us a favor.

S: What would you like us to do for you, Mrs. Zhang?

Z: And as you know, our main office is a new office, so currently we don't have enough time or staff to invite potential clients. Could you help us with this?

S: Of course. You could just give us an effective target client list, according to your market, and then we will invite them for you free of charge.

Z: Wonderful. Thanks.

S: My pleasure. And, all that we've just discussed can be written in the exhibition contract.

Z: Yes. Let's move forward with the contract.

Vocabulary

publication	[ˌpʌblɪˈkeɪʃn]	n.	出版；发表
commit	[kəˈmɪt]	v.	把……交托给；使……承担义务
dedicate	[ˈdedɪkeɪt]	v.	致力；献身
pertain	[pəˈteɪn]	v.	关于；适合

Notes

1. I'd be very happy to give you any further information you need.
   我非常乐意提供您所需的任何信息。

2. What would you like us to do for you?
   您希望我们为您做什么？

3. move forward with 推进

4. free of charge 免费

Useful Sentences 常用口语

1. I'm pleased to invite you to be our exhibitor.
   我很高兴您成为我们的参展商。

2. I hope you can join us for the show.
   我希望你们能参加这次展会。

3. What time would be good for you?
   您认为什么时间合适?

4. We will take into account the needs of exhibitors.
   我们会考虑参展商的需要。

5. We ensure close cooperation.
   我们确保密切合作。

6. Could I visit you at your company?
   是否方便到贵公司拜访您?

7. I think we may be able to cooperate in the future.
   我想也许将来我们可以合作。

8. The trade show provides a unique opportunity for all exhibitors to meet, expand their circle of communication, establish partnerships, and conduct new business.
   这次展会为参展商提供了独特的机会。行业人士可以借此与同行会晤、拓展交际圈、建立合作伙伴关系、开展新业务。

9. By attending our show, participants efficiently, effectively and productively gain immediate competitive advantages for their business and stay abreast with the latest developments in the industry.
   通过参加我们的展会,企业可以成功、有效地赢得即时的竞争优势,与行业的最新发展保持同步。

10. It is a five-day exhibition that brings together worldwide buyers and sellers from every sector of the MICE industry.
    这是一个为期5天的展会,届时来自世界各地的会展业相关的买卖双方将汇聚一堂。

11. We have been working closely with relevant professional bodies, trade associations and government departments. And we ensure that each exhibition is targeted and related industry needs.
    我们一直与相关的专业机构、贸易协会和政府部门紧密合作,确保每一次的展会都能符合行业的需要。

🔗 Further Reading 拓展阅读

【拓展音频】

Most salesmen are naturally competitive. It's what makes them good at what they do. They are driven by numbers, goals and rewards, and are accustomed to frequent public reports on their progress, as well as that of their colleagues. Therefore, your event-invitation goals, with friendly competition, can motivate a salesman to make customer invitations a priority.

To make your invitation efforts into an effective competition, firstly learn why your sales representatives aren't currently supporting your event's program. Do they not find the content or agenda compelling, and therefore believe the event will not be interesting to their customers? Are they convinced that their customers will not attend? Why? Are they too busy with daily sales-calls, customer-care, and administrative requirements and they simply do not have enough time to add another to-do item to their lists? Once you have this insight, you can modify your event and invitation strategy to help gain sales buy-in and support.

Next, work with sales managers to develop the goals and incentive structure for your invitation program. invitation managers in this important step will ensure they are on board with your concept, and will give it their support. Ask them to set minimum invitation goals for their sales representatives (for example, each representative must send 10 invitations, with a goal of getting at least six clients to accept and attend the event). If managers communicate the goals and incentive structure with their sales representatives, the representatives will be more likely to embrace the task and support the event.

Be sure you have an incentive that appeals to your sales team. For example, a sales representative who lures the most quality clients and prospects to an event wins four tickets to a local sporting game, or a night out to dinner. Sales managers will most likely support this effort, and keep a running tally of the standings. Announcing the results at a weekly sales meeting will hopefully energize the representatives, and increase attendance at the event. While short-term prize incentives can motivate a sales team, and long-term or built-in incentives can be even more influential. For example, some managers may be willing to include representatives' success on event-related goals as a part of their performance ratings—or even as a part of their annual compensation plans.

Also look for success stories tied to previous events. Did a sales representative close a sale as a result of meeting with a prospect or customer at an event? Peer-to-peer exchanges can only help your efforts to drive participation and support.

Lastly, develop a post-event strategy to help sales follow up. Create an offer, a unique opportunity or a piece of information that you can deliver to all attendees after the event. Sales Reps will then have a natural hook to follow-up potential prospects: "What did you think of the information we sent to you after the event?" Now, you've not only created an exciting event, and gotten sales excited to participate, you've also ensured a follow-up opportunity that can help the Reps shorten their sales cycle, which benefits you both.

Vocabulary

reward	[rɪˈwɔːd]	n.	报酬；酬谢
accustom	[əˈkʌstəm]	v.	使习惯于
frequent	[ˈfriːkwənt]	adj.	频繁的
colleague	[ˈkɒliːg]	n.	同事
motivate	[ˈməʊtɪveɪt]	v.	使有动机
priority	[praɪˈɒrəti]	n.	优先；优先权
agenda	[əˈdʒendə]	n.	议程
compelling	[kəmˈpelɪŋ]	adj.	激发兴趣的
convince	[kənˈvɪns]	v.	使信服
administrative	[ədˈmɪnɪstrətɪv]	adj.	管理的
structure	[ˈstrʌktʃə(r)]	n.	结构
embrace	[ɪmˈbreɪs]	v.	拥抱
appeal	[əˈpiːl]	v.	有吸引力
lure	[lʊə(r)]	n.	诱惑
tally	[ˈtæli]	n.	计数器
influential	[ˌɪnfluˈenʃl]	adj.	有影响的

Notes

1. They are driven by numbers, goals and rewards, and are accustomed to frequent public reports on their progress, as well as that of their colleagues.

他们都被数字、目标和回报所驱动，并且习惯于频繁公开报告他们及其同事们的进展情况。

2. Therefore, your event-invitation goals, with friendly competition, can motivate a salesman to make customer invitations a priority.

因此，你的活动邀请目标及友好的竞争，能够激励销售人员把客户邀请放在优先地位。

3. Do they not find the content or agenda compelling, and therefore believe the event will not be interesting to their customers?

难道他们没有发现感兴趣的内容和议程，并且因此认为活动不会令他们的客户感兴趣？

4. Are they too busy with daily sales-calls, customer-care, and administrative requirements and simply do not have enough time to add another to-do item to their lists?

他们是忙于每天的销售电话、客户服务、管理要求，而根本就没有足够的时间在日程表中增加另外一个活动项目吗？

5. For example, some managers may be willing to include representatives' success on event-related goals as a part of their performance ratings—or even as a part of their annual compensation plans.

例如，一些管理者可能会把代表们能否成功实现相关活动目标作为他们业绩评级的标准——或者甚至把这当成是评定年度奖金方案的条件之一。

6. Peer-to-peer exchanges can only help your efforts to drive participation and support.

同行之间的交流可以在促进合作与支持方面助你一臂之力。

7. Sales Reps will then have a natural hook to follow-up potential prospects: "What did you think of the information we sent to you after the event?"

销售代表自然对潜在客户进行随访："您如何评价我们在活动后向您发送的信息？"

Answer the following questions.

1. What is the main topic of this passage?
2. What can be the best title of this passage?

Decide whether the following statements are True or False based on the above passage.

1. Salesmen will not usually invite customers without setting invitation goals.　　　　（　）

2. If you modify your event and invitation strategy according to what sales representatives think, you will most likely get their support, and promote sales.　　　　（　）

3. You should ask sales representatives to set minimum invitation goals.　　　　（　）

4. Compared with long-term incentives, short-term incentives, such as prizes, can be even more influential. (   )

5. Peer-to-peer exchanges can only help your efforts to drive participation and support. (   )

6. A post-event strategy can benefit participants as well as event organizers. (   )

Exercises

1. Match the words on the left with their proper meaning on the right.

(1) remind   a. a successful attempt at scoring
(2) research   b. the financial assistance in time of need
(3) region   c. a catch for locking a door
(4) hook   d. the extended spatial location of something
(5) benefit   e. a search for knowledge
(6) goal   f. put in the mind of someone
(7) event   g. make someone agree on something
(8) support   h. an earnest or urgent request
(9) appeal   i. aiding the cause or policy or interests of
(10) convince   j. something that happens at a given place and time

2. Read the following statements, and fill in the blank spaces with the appropriate words contained in the word box.

| show   visit   attract   products   invitation   audience |

(1) Participating in a trade show is a great way to introduce your company and your _____.

(2) There's a lot to think about when planning for a trade _____.

(3) It is important to remember that the _____ is really the start of your trade show's success and deserves just as much time and efforts other aspects do.

(4) An invitation that is well-designed, unique, and interactive will increase attendance because you have engaged your _____ from the very beginning.

(5) Use the power of word-of-mouth to _____ attendees.

(6) Your message on an eye-catching invitation will attract your ideal customers and motivate them to _____ your booth.

3. Translate the following sentences into English.

(1) 我们会充分考虑参展商的需要的。

(2) 这次展会为参展商提供了独特的商业机会。

(3) 通过参加我们的展会，企业可以成功、有效地为自身赢得竞争优势。

(4) 我希望你们能参加这次国际进出口贸易展会。

4. Role play.

Make up a dialogue based on the following situation.

Suppose you are an assistant of China International Auto Parts Expo. You are calling one of your regular customers to invite him to attend your show from Oct. 26th, 2012 to Oct. 28th, 2012.

Practical Training Project 实训项目

Search the Internet to locate a trade show that is suitable for your company to exhibit your products. Prepare a 10-minute presentation introducing the show, and explain why your company should participate in this show.

Unit 4

Choice of Venues
场 馆 选 择

Unit 4
场馆选择
Choice of Venues

Learning Objectives 学习目标

After learning this unit, you will be able to:
★ Make a checklist before choosing a venue.
★ Discuss the venue with your partner.
★ Know the importance of choosing an exhibition venue.
★ Master the useful expressions and sentences concerning this topic.

Background Information 背景知识

展览场地的选择是展会成功举办的重要因素。一般来说,展览场地需要充足的免费停车位,举行展览的区域必须符合展示的规模。在一个大型区域举行小型的展会,会让人感觉很空旷和冷清;在小型区域举行大型的展会,则会让人觉得拥挤和不舒服,从而导致观众提早离开会场,参展商也会认为展会举办得不成功。因此,展览场地的选择应该慎之又慎。

Lead-in 导入活动

The choice of a venue is a critical factor for the success of the exhibition. Choosing the most appropriate venue, that works well for you, is the first step towards making a successful event.

【拓展视频】

When you are choosing a venue, the facts you should consider can range from the appearance of the venue, the surrounding, the equipment and furniture even to the cleanness of the toilets.

So make sure that you are well prepared to make good decisions and get the most out of your event.

Warm-up 热身活动

Match and Discuss

Directions: Match the pictures in the left column with the corresponding terms in the right column, and discuss with your partner to see how much you understand about the choice of venues.

1.    A. make a checklist before choosing a venue

2.    B. choose the appropriate venue

3.    C. write an exhibition report

4.    D. discuss the venue with your partner

Unit 4

场馆选择
Choice of Venues

Basic Reading 基础阅读

How to Choose the Perfect Venue for Your Business Exhibition?

Putting on an exhibition can be an exciting job. But if you choose the wrong venue, then your hard work could be wasted, and the excitement will soon be replaced with stress and disappointment. A wrong choice may even be damaging to your company reputation. Therefore, follow our top five recommendations on choosing the perfect exhibition venue.

1. Set of Your Budget

Always start by knowing your budget. Check what extras are not included in the quoted price; don't assume everything you need is included. Prepare a detailed list of your requirements and take it to your first meeting, or e-mail the list to event coordinators to help them prepare for the meeting.

2. Size & Location

Don't waste time looking at venues that are beyond your budget range. Next, to budget correctly, think carefully about the size of the venue you will need. Determine the maximum number of people you think will be attending—always better to over allocate space.

Don't forget to look at the parking facilities, if it is free. You need to ensure that there is adequate parking at the exhibition venue, or at least close by.

3. Onsite Facilities

Look at the facilities available at the venue. Will you be holding seminars and workshops at your exhibition? Are there separate breakout rooms for this? Does the venue have enough washroom facilities to avoid lengthy queues during breaks?

You can consider hiring technical aids, but it's worth checking if the venue will include aids in the contract. Some venues have state-of-the-art rooms and equipment— this could save you money and relieve the headache of sourcing external suppliers.

4. Catering

A key consideration for any events is catering, both in terms of availability and quality. Research what your considered venue can provide. Everything from the quality of the china, to the choice of coffee and the variety of foods available is important. Catering provided by the venue is usually a superior quality than an external caterer. Cost is also likely to be very competitive. Why? The venue will have a reputation to protect in terms of quality, cost and service.

5. Local Area

It is vital to consider what amenities are available in the local area, such as hotels and transportation (airports, trains, buses and taxi services). This is extremely important should your exhibition take longer than planned. You need to make it easy for exhibitors and visitors to get to and from the venue. Also, check with local hotels to determine if they have special discounted exhibition rates that can be offered to your visitors.

Vocabulary

disappointment	[ˌdɪsəˈpɔɪntmənt]	n.	失望
quote	[kwəʊt]	v.	报价
allocate	[ˈæləkeɪt]	v.	分配
facility	[fəˈsɪləti]	n.	设施
available	[əˈveɪləbl]	adj.	可利用的
seminar	[ˈsemɪnɑː(r)]	n.	讨论会
separate	[ˈseprət]	adj.	单独的，分开的
breakout	[ˈbreɪkaʊt]	n.	爆发
lengthy	[ˈleŋθi]	adj.	漫长的
queue	[kjuː]	n.	队列
external	[ɪkˈstɜːnl]	adj.	外部的
amenity	[əˈmiːnəti]	n.	便利设施

Notes

1. Determine the maximum number of people you think will be attending—always better to

over allocate space.

确定你认为的将会出席的总人数——通常要安排充足的场地。

2. Some venues have state-of-the-art rooms and equipment—this could save you money and relieve the headache of sourcing external suppliers.

有些场馆拥有最先进的展室和设备——这样可以为你节省费用，还可以省去寻找外部供应商这类头疼的事。

3. It is vital to consider what amenities are available in the local area, such as hotels and transportation.

最重要的是要考虑一下在当地有什么可以利用的便利设施，如酒店和交通。

4. Also, check with local hotels to determine if they have special discounted exhibition rates that can be offered to your visitors.

此外，与当地酒店核实，确定他们是否有特殊折扣的展会房价可以提供给你的参观者。

Discuss the following questions with your partner.

1. Work in groups of two or more, and discuss with your partner about the five recommendations on choosing the exhibition venue.

2. What are your opinions and suggestions on this topic?

3. When you choose an exhibition venue, and what factors should you consider?

Situational Dialogues 情景对话

【拓展术语】

Dialogue 1

Lucy Li (an exhibition manager of Asia Natural Luxury Woolen Product Co., Ltd) is considering choosing a trade show venue with Mr. Yang (sales representative of the upcoming Shanghai International Luxury Trade Show).

Y=Mr. Yang   L= Lucy Li

Y: Good morning, madam. How can I help you?

L: Yes, please call me Lucy. Our company is planning to exhibit our luxury woolen product at an international trade show. Where do you think would be a good location for a luxury exhibition?

Y: I am afraid that developing areas may not be ideal.

L: Do you mean that people can't afford to purchase luxury items in those areas?

Y: Compared with those in the developed cities, people in the developing areas have less purchasing power.

L: I see. Then it would be better to hold our trade show in developed cities.

Y: That would be much better. As you know, people's living standards in different cities are quite varied. Cities like Beijing and Shanghai are more economically developed.

L: So, you mean it would be better to hold our first exhibition in Beijing or Shanghai?

Y: That's right. I suggest we consider Shanghai. Since it's an international metropolis, I think there will be more target clients.

L: Sounds good. But where would be the venue for the show? I am not familiar with Shanghai.

Y: There are many exhibition halls in Shanghai. I think the most popular one is the Shanghai International Exhibition Center.

L: Good, that would be a very nice venue. Maybe we can arrange some time to have an onsite visit.

Y: Sure!

Vocabulary

luxury	[ˈlʌkʃəri]	adj.	奢侈的
woolen	[ˈwʊlən]	adj.	羊毛的
standard	[ˈstændəd]	n.	标准
onsite	[ˈɒnsaɪt]	adj.	在场的
metropolis	[məˈtrɒpəlɪs]	n.	大都市
economically	[ˌiːkəˈnɒmɪkli]	ad.	在经济上

Notes

1. Where do you think would be a good location for a luxury exhibition?
   你认为对于奢侈品展会来说选择什么样的展会地点比较好呢？

2. Do you mean that people can't afford to purchase luxury items in those areas?
   你是说那些地区的人们买不起奢侈品？

3. compared with 与……相比

   For example: Compared with those in the developed cities, people in the developing areas have less purchasing power.
   例如：与发达城市相比，发展中地区人们的消费能力确实要弱一些。

4. As you know, people's living standards in different cities are quite varied.
   你知道，不同城市的人的生活水平也大不相同。

5. Cities such as Beijing and Shanghai are more economically developed.
   像北京和上海这样的城市，经济要发达得多。

6. Since it's an international metropolis, I think there will be more target clients.
   作为国际化大都市，我想那里会有更多的目标客户。

Dialogue 2

S=staff   J=John

S: Good morning, this is the Beijing International Exhibition Center.

J: Good Morning, this is John. I'd like to ask you some questions about holding a fashion show in your place.

S: Hello, John. What would you like to know?

J: Have you had many exhibitions in your place before?

S: Yes. We've had many shows at our venue, including foods, fashions, wines, jewelries, furniture, and many more. What are you going to display at the show?

J: We plan to display modern design fashion clothing. We will need an area about 400m^2 with separate small booths.

S: So a medium-sized exhibition hall will be right for you.

J: Good. Thank you for your recommendation.

Vocabulary

furniture	[ˈfɜːnɪtʃə(r)]	n.	家具
medium	[ˈmiːdiəm]	adj.	中等的
separate	[ˈseprət]	adj.	单独的，分开的
fashion	[ˈfæʃn]	n.	时尚；时装

Notes

1. I'd like to ask you some questions about holding a fashion show in your place.
   我想问一下关于在贵地举行时装展的事宜。

2. What would you like to know?
   您想了解哪方面信息？

3. What are you going to display at the show?
   您准备在展会上展示什么产品？

4. Modern design fashion clothing.
   最新设计的时装。

5. So a medium-sized exhibition hall will be right for you.
   那么，一个中型展厅会适合您。

【拓展音频】

Useful Sentences 常用口语

1. Have you thought of a good location for this trade show?
   你想到办商展的最佳地点了吗？
2. So before choosing a venue, you'd better make a checklist about the particular requirements of your exhibition.
   所以在选择展会前，你最好为展会的详细要求列一个清单。
3. And then it's also important for you to have an on-site inspection of the venue.
   然后你还应该进行一次实地考察，这也很重要。
4. If the venue is too small, it will leave the participants feeling congested and uncomfortable.
   如果展会地点过于狭窄，会让参展者觉得拥挤、不舒服。
5. If the venue is too big, it may leave the participants an impression that the exhibition is not as popular as they have expected.
   如果展会过于空旷，则会给参展者留下展会不像他们预期的那样受欢迎和繁忙的印象。
6. The factors you should consider can range from the appearance of the venue, the surroundings, the equipment and the furniture, even to the cleanness of the toilets.
   总而言之，你需要考虑的因素，大到展会地点的外观、周边环境，小到设施、家具，甚至卫生间的清洁程度。
7. Choosing a suitable exhibition venue is one of the first things that you should consider during your preparation time.
   选择合适的展会地点是展会准备首先要考虑的事情。
8. To find out the most suitable venue is not an easy task.
   找到一个合适的展会地点不是一件容易的事。
9. What exhibition facilities can you use in the venue?
   展会地点有哪些会展设施可以利用？
10. How convenient is the transportation?
    交通是否便利？
11. How about the cost?
    花费如何？
12. Are there any suitable hotels near the venue?
    展会地点附近有没有合适的酒店？

Further Reading 拓展阅读

Beijing International Exhibition Center

Founded in 1985, Beijing International Exhibition Centre (BIEC) is a professional exhibition-organizing department under CCPIT Beijing (CCOIC Beijing). The predecessor of

Unit 4
场 馆 选 择
Choice of Venues

BIEC was the Exhibition Department of CCPIT Beijing, which was one of the organizations with the longest history in organizing international exhibitions both at home and abroad.

BIEC has successfully organized 180 international exhibitions in China since 1978, which attracts more than 15 000 companies and manufacturers from 30 countries and regions, including large and medium-sized enterprises. These exhibitions have included the areas of transportation, power & energy, sound & music instruments, refrigeration & air-conditioning, military logistics, elevators, real estate, etc. These exhibitions have greatly improved the development of those relevant industries. Many have become the most influential international professional forums in China, and have a very high reputation in the international exhibition industry. At present, all the exhibitions organized by BIEC have developed into periodic professional exhibitions. At the same time, BIEC has opened up a new way to combine together exhibition, trade and technical seminars, by inviting outside investment and market exploration, thereby providing broader space for both Chinese and foreign enterprises to promote economic, and technology exchanges and cooperation in various fields.

BIEC has also arranged for many import and export corporations and industrial & commercial enterprises, most of which are from Beijing, to hold exhibitions abroad, with participation in more than 50 international exhibitions and fairs in 30 countries and regions of the world. BIEC has made great contributions to the mutual understanding between China and other countries, and has enhanced the development of China's foreign trade.

Over the years, Beijing International Exhibition Centre has amassed a vast experience in organizing exhibitions, with a large number of qualified and competent staff. BIEC strives to provide high-quality exhibition services to deliver exchange, cooperation and development between China and foreign countries in all fields.

Vocabulary

instrument	['ɪnstrəmənt]	n.	仪器
refrigeration	[rɪˌfrɪdʒə'reɪʃ(ə)n]	n.	制冷
military	['mɪlətri]	adj.	军事的
estate	[ɪ'steɪt]	n.	房地产
influential	[ˌɪnflu'enʃl]	adj.	有影响的
combine	[kəm'baɪn]	v.	结合
seminar	['semɪnɑː(r)]	n.	讨论会
exploration	[ˌeksplə'reɪʃn]	n.	探测，探索
mutual	['mjuːtʃuəl]	adj.	共同的
exchange	[ɪks'tʃeɪndʒ]	n.	交换
strive	[straɪv]	v.	努力；奋斗
competent	['kɒmpɪtənt]	adj.	胜任的

Notes

1. BIEC: Beijing International Exhibition Centre 北京国际展览中心
2. CCPIT: China Council for the Promotion of International Trade 中国国际贸易促进委员会
3. CCOIC: China Chamber of International Commerce 中国国际商会
4. The predecessor of BIEC was the Exhibition Department of CCPIT Beijing, which was one of the organizations with the longest history in organizing international exhibitions both at home and abroad.
   北京国际展览中心的前身是中国国际贸易促进委员会北京展览部，这是在国内外举办国际性展览历史最悠久的组织之一。
5. Thereby providing broader space for both Chinese and foreign enterprises to promote economic, and technology exchanges and cooperation in various fields.
   从而为中外企业提供更广阔的空间，促进各个领域的经济、技术交流与合作。
6. BIEC has also arranged for many import and export corporations and industrial & commercial enterprises, most of which are from Beijing, to hold exhibitions abroad, with participation in more than 50 international exhibitions and fairs in 30 countries and regions of the world.

Unit 4
场馆选择
Choice of Venues

北京国际会展中心已经为许多进出口公司和工商企业，其中大部分是来自北京的企业，安排了到国外举办展览，参与了在世界 30 个国家和地区举办的 50 多场国际展览会和交易会。

7. Over the years, Beijing International Exhibition Centre has amassed a vast experience in organizing exhibitions, with a large mumber of qualified and competent staff.

在过去的几年中，北京国际会展中心已经积累了丰富的办展经验，拥有一大批高素质、有实力的员工。

Answer the following questions.

1. When we choose an exhibition center to hold an exhibition, which factors should we consider?

2. How much do you know about Beijing International Exhibition Center? Give us a brief introduction about it.

Decide if the following statements are True or False based on the above passage.

1. The predecessor of BIEC was the Exhibition Department of CCPIT Beijing, which was one of the organizations with the shortest history in organizing international exhibitions both at home and abroad.   (   )

2. To some degree, these exhibitions have improved the development of those relevant industries.   (   )

3. At present, all the exhibitions organized by BIEC have developed into annual professional exhibitions.   (   )

4. Meanwhile, BIEC has opened up a new way to combine together exhibition, trade and technical seminars, by inviting outside investment and market exploration.   (   )

5. Thereby providing broader space for Chinese enterprises to promote economic, and technology exchanges and cooperation in various fields.   (   )

6. BIEC strives to provide high-quality exhibition services to deliver exchange, cooperation and development between China and foreign countries in all fields.   (   )

Exercises

1. Match the words on the left with their proper meaning on the right.

(1) choose   a. to exert much effort or energy

(2) venue   b. supply food ready to eat; for parties and banquets

(3) reputation   c. a line of people or vehicles waiting for something

(4) extra   d. the act of grasping

(5) assume   e. an area in which something acts

(6) range   f. take to be the case or to be true

(7) hold   g. more than is needed, desired or required

(8) queue   h. the state of being held in high esteem and honor

(9) cater   i. the scene of any events or actions

(10) strive   j. pick out from a number of alternatives

2. Read the following statements and fill in the blanks with the appropriate words in the word box.

type	consider	inspection	venue	takes	important

(1) One of the most _____ factors in the overall success of your event is your choice of venue.

(2) To find the most appropriate venue _____ time.

(3) Choosing an exhibition _____ doesn't have to be overwhelming. It's actually a fun challenge.

(4) Let's assume you have already identified the _____ of event you are planning and its purpose.

(5) Now you have many other factors to _____ as you select the venue itself.

(6) Every event planner should conduct a site _____ before finally deciding on a particular venue.

3. Translate the following sentences into English.

(1) 在选择展会前,你最好为展会的详细要求列一个清单。

(2) 如果展会地点过于狭窄,会让参展者觉得拥挤、不舒服。

(3) 选择合适的展会地点是展会准备过程中首先要考虑的事情。

(4) 选择一个合适的展会地点不是一件容易的事。

4. Role play.

(1) Suppose you are a clerk working at a convention center, how will you introduce your center to a visitor?

(2) Suppose you are a planner of an exhibition, how will you choose a proper exposition center?

 Practical Training Project 实训项目

Research and review a recent trade show report on the Internet. Prepare a 10-minute presentation, indicating the reasons why this venue may have been selected, and the potential advantages realized by the exhibiting company.

Unit 5

Attending an Exhibition
参 加 展 览

Unit 5
参加展览 ATTENDING AN EXHIBITION

Learning Objectives 学习目标

After learning this unit, you will be able to:

★ Know the proper procedures for companies or enterprises, and individuals to attend an exhibition.

★ Introduce and promote an exhibition.

★ Know how to inquire about an exhibition.

★ Master some useful professional words, phrases and key sentence patterns.

Background Information 背景知识

企业参展是一个系统性很强的工作，不仅要根据企业市场营销规划从宏观上把握好展会的选择、参展流程控制，而且要从细节上做好诸如展位选择、展品策划、现场管理等工作。

Lead-in 导入活动

【拓展视频】

Many companies now see industry events like exhibitions and trade fairs as a key aspect of their marketing strategies. More businesses are now aware of the impact that effective exhibition displays at these events and their relative advantages over traditional advertising such as television or print media.

◇ **Large Target Audience**

In terms of resources, exhibition represents a far more economical option than traditional forms of advertising, which may be ignored and provide little or no positive return at all.

◇ **Affordable Cost**

Exhibiting at an event is a cost-effective alternative to most other promotional strategies, as resources such as exhibition stands are relatively inexpensive.

◇ **Interaction**

Exhibitions and trade fairs provide the opportunity for you to directly interact with an interested and enquiring public.

Warm-up 热身活动

Match and Discuss

Directions: Match the pictures in the left column with the activities in the right column, and discuss with your partner to determine how much you understand about the activities of attending an exhibition.

1.    A. sign the contracts

2.    B. make direct eye contact

Unit 5
参加展览
Attending an Exhibition

3. C. exchange business cards

4. D. introduce an auto show

 Basic Reading 基础阅读

If your company wants to attend an exhibition, such as the China Jilin Northeast Asia Investment and Trade Exposition (also called Northeast Asia Expo), what should you do? Just tell the sponsor that you want to attend the exhibition and then submit the money? NO! Actually there are many procedures to deal with prior to attending an exhibition.

Let me explain how to attend the exhibition.

Firstly, you should submit an application for attending the exhibition. You obtain the application form from your local chamber of commerce, or from the official exhibition website. Then mail the application form to the local chamber of commerce, or submit the form online. Submit the form within the required time period! Of course, if you are a foreign enterprise or individual, don't forget to apply for a visa. Then you must wait for the exhibition staff to verify the validity of the information you have submitted. Secondly (after your application has been accepted), according to your requirements, reserve a booth and confirm the area or position for your display. Then you must submit a monetary deposit for your booth. Thirdly, give the information concerning your company or enterprise and the type of exhibit to the sponsor. Fourthly, apply for drawings, the use of electricity, telephone requirements and any other necessities, to successfully display your goods at the exhibition. Then submit payment for the relevant expenses for the exhibition. This means that you are now ready to participate in the exhibition.

Vocabulary

sponsor	['spɒnsə(r)]	n.	主办者
procedure	[prə'siːdʒə(r)]	n.	程序
application	[ˌæplɪ'keɪʃn]	n.	应用
chamber	['tʃeɪmbə(r)]	n.	会场
commerce	['kɒmɜːs]	n.	商业
submit	[səb'mɪt]	v.	提交
visa	['viːzə]	n.	签证
verify	['verɪfaɪ]	v.	证明；核实
validity	[və'lɪdəti]	n.	有效
requirement	[rɪ'kwaɪəmənt]	n.	要求
confirm	[kən'fɜːm]	v.	确认
deposit	[dɪ'pɒzɪt]	n.	保证金
electricity	[ɪˌlek'trɪsəti]	n.	电力
modification	[ˌmɒdɪfɪ'keɪʃn]	n.	修改
relevant	['reləvənt]	adj.	相关联的
expense	[ɪk'spens]	n.	费用

Notes

1. China-Northeast Asia Investment and Trade Exposition, also called Northeast Asia Expo.
   中国吉林东北亚投资贸易博览会，又称东北亚博览会。

Unit 5

参 加 展 览
Attending an Exhibition

2. Actually there are many procedures to deal with prior to attending an exhibition.
   实际上，在参加展会之前有许多手续要办理。

3. You obtain the application form from your local chamber of commerce, or from the official exhibition website.
   你从当地的商会或展会的官方网站索取申请表格。

4. Then you must wait for the exhibition staff to verify the validity of the information you have submitted.
   然后，你必须等待展会工作人员验证你所提交信息的有效性。

5. Thirdly, give the information concerning your company or enterprise and the type of exhibit to the sponsor.
   第三，把贵公司或企业的相关信息和展品类型提供给主办方。

6. Fourthly, apply for drawings, the use of electricity, telephone requirements and any other necessities, to successfully display your goods at the exhibition.
   第四，申请图纸、用电、电话服务及一切其他必需品，在展会上成功地展示你的商品。

Discuss the following question with your partner.

What are the procedures for attending an exhibition? Make a list.

【拓展术语】

Situational Dialogues 情景对话

Dialogue 1

A: Good afternoon, Changchun International Expo Center. May I help you?

B: I'd like to participate in the 7th Changchun International Auto Expo. But I have no idea about the participation procedures. Could you please give me some details?

A: Thank you for making the decision to join us, Sir. In order to make exhibitors' registration as easy as possible, we offer three convenient registration methods-on line, by fax, or by mail.

B: How can I obtain the registration form?

A: If you'd like to register on line, you can simply complete and submit online registration. If you'd like to register by fax or mail, you may download the registration form from our Internet website, and then fax or mail the completed form to us.

B: How could I know you have received my registration form?

A: Confirmation by e-mail or a written confirmation will be sent to you within 15 days of receipt according to the registration form.

B: OK, but when should I submit payment?

A: Your payment must follow within a week.

B: Thank you for your excellent explanation.

A: You are very welcome.

Vocabulary

procedure	[prə'siːdʒə(r)]	n.	程序
registration	[ˌredʒɪ'streɪʃn]	n.	登记
offer	['ɒfə(r)]	v.	提供
convenient	[kən'viːniənt]	adj.	方便的
receive	[rɪ'siːv]	v.	收到
confirmation	[ˌkɒnfə'meɪʃn]	n.	确认
receipt	[rɪ'siːt]	n.	收据
payment	['peɪmənt]	n.	付款

Notes

1. Changchun International Expo Center 长春国际会展中心

2. I'd like to participate in the 7th Changchun International Auto Expo.
   我打算参加第七届长春国际汽车博览会。

3. But I have no idea about the participation procedures.
   但是我对参展程序一无所知。

4. in order to 为了……
   For example: In order to make exhibitors' registration as easy as possible, we offer three convenient registration methods: on line, by fax, or by mail.
   例如：为了方便参展商登记，我们提供 3 种便利的登记方式：网上登记、传真登记和邮件登记。

5. registration form 登记表

【拓展音频】

6. Confirmation by e-mail or a written confirmation will be sent to you within 15 days of receipt of the registration form.
   （组委会）将在收到您的参展报名表后的 15 天之内，以电子邮件或书面形式把《参展确认通知书》寄给您。

Unit 5
参 加 展 览
ATTENDING an Exhibition

Dialogue 2

A: Good afternoon, Changchun International Expo Center. How may I assist you?

B: Good afternoon. I'm very interested in participating in the 8th China Jilin Northeast Asia Investment and Trade Exposition. Can you give me some information about the participation procedure? What options are available to submit my exhibition registration form?

A: Thank you very much for your support and participation. There are three registration methods: on line, by mail, or by fax. If you'd like to register by mail or by fax, please log on to the following website (www.ccicec.com) to download the detailed materials and various forms. Then you can fax or mail the form to us when completed, and be sure to submit your registration form within three weeks prior to the Trade Exposition. If you want to register on line, you can simply submit online registration form.

B: Thank you for your explanation. How can I confirm my participation?

A: After we have received the participation form, we will send you a confirmation letter.

B: Thank you very much.

A: You're welcome. If you require any other information or special assistance, please feel free to contact us.

Vocabulary

option	['ɒpʃn]	n.	选项；选择权
available	[ə'veɪləbl]	adj.	有效的；可利用的
method	['meθəd]	n.	方法
material	[mə'tɪəriəl]	n.	材料
various	['veəriəs]	adj.	各种各样的
complete	[kəm'pliːt]	adj.	完全的
require	[rɪ'kwaɪə(r)]	v.	需要
assistance	[ə'sɪstəns]	n.	帮助

Notes

1. the 8th China Jilin Northeast Asia Investment and Trade Exposition
   第八届中国吉林东北亚投资贸易博览会

2. log on 登录
   For example: please log on the exhibition website.
   例如：请登录这个展会网站。

3. detailed materials 详细资料

4. How can I confirm my participation?
   怎样确认我的参展资格呢？

5. After we received the participation form, we will send you a confirmation letter.
   在收到参展表格后，我们会把《参展确认通知书》寄给您。

6. If you require any other information or special assistance, please feel free to contact us.
   如果需要其他方面的信息或特别的帮助，尽管联系我们。

【拓展音频】

Useful Sentences 常用口语

1. Thank you again for your participation.
   再次感谢您的参与。

2. Will you require a standard booth or an open space?
   您是要标准展位还是一块空地？

3. It is really wise of you to choose such a good place.
   选择这样一个好地方真是明智之举。

4. Could you tell me something about the booth rental?
   你能告诉我有关场租费的情况吗？

5. The principles of booth allocation still are "apply first, pay first, and get served first".
   展位安排原则仍是"先预订，先付款，先安排"。

6. I have no idea about the participation procedure.
   我对于参展程序一无所知。

7. Can you give me some details about the participation procedure?
   您可以就参展程序提供一些详细的情况吗？

8. How can I obtain the registration form?
   我怎样得到登记表格？

9. How may I help you?
   有什么需要帮忙的吗？

10. I would like to know more about your exhibition agenda.
    我想了解一下更多的展览会日程。

11. When can we construct the booth?
    我们什么时候搭建展台呢？

12. What time will the opening ceremony be held?
    开幕式什么时候举行？

13. When shall we dismantle the booth?
    什么时候拆除展位呢？

Unit 5
参加展览 Attending an Exhibition

🔗 Further Reading 拓展阅读

The benefits of attending trade shows and exhibitions are numerous. If you are planning to promote your products or services, attending an exhibition, or a trade show, is a wise decision. Whether you are a wholesaler, manufacturer, distributor, customer, retailer or drop shipper, you cannot ignore the importance of attending this type of event. You will realize numerous resources and opportunities in a single event.

The benefits of attending trade shows and exhibitions include getting potential customers, information on the most active products, current pricing, and other market opportunities. In short, you can get all the information about the products, customers and competitors under one roof. Moreover, you can get wide exposure of your market because every businessman related to the industry is present and looking for the best deals for their business.

The following are just a few of the wide array of benefits when attending these kinds of events.

※ **Wide Exposure**

Attending a trade show will increase your exposure to your respective industry. This is beneficial in the sense that it can help increase the public awareness with regards to your product offerings and services. You can get many direct contacts by just attending an exhibition or trade show. By following up with these contacts, you can convert them to leads and then into long-term customers. It also creates favorable impression among the attendees, in knowing that you are personally visiting them at the event.

※ **Further Sales Lead**

You can also be more competitive in the sense that you can increase your sales leads. As a sales person, it is your responsibility to transform the prospect into a customer. Through the exhibitions, you can increase your client-base which will enhance your sales.

※ **Face-to-Face Interaction**

According to experts, the main purpose of attending exhibitions or trade shows is to gain personal interaction with the prospective clients. You cannot get this medium of interaction by simply using online B2B sites and other promotional mediums. Your personal interaction and presence can help you to get direct feedback for your products and services. You can also directly answer all questions that prospective customers might ask about your company.

※ **Survey of Latest Market Trends**

Attending the trade show will work as a survey for you to know the latest market trends in your industry. You will be able to know the viability of your products and services as well. If you are new into the market, you will be able to learn the techniques on how to penetrate the market, identify the needs, market visibility and other useful information. You can also know the appropriate marketing strategies to use in your particular industry.

Vocabulary

wholesaler	[ˈhəʊlseɪlə(r)]	n.	批发商
manufacturer	[ˌmænjuˈfæktʃərə(r)]	n.	制造商
distributor	[dɪˈstrɪbjətə(r)]	n.	分销商
retailer	[ˈriːteɪlə(r)]	n.	零售商
exposure	[ɪkˈspəʊʒə(r)]	n.	曝光，亮相
array	[əˈreɪ]	n.	队列；一大批
respective	[rɪˈspektɪv]	adj.	各自的
awareness	[əˈweənəs]	n.	意识
convert	[kənˈvɜːt]	v.	（使）转变
transform	[trænsˈfɔːm]	v.	改变
prospect	[ˈprɒspekt]	n.	前景
interaction	[ˌɪntərˈækʃən]	n.	互相影响
viability	[ˌvaɪəˈbɪlɪti]	n.	生存能力
penetrate	[ˈpenətreɪt]	v.	渗入
visibility	[ˌvɪzəˈbɪləti]	n.	能见度

Unit 5
参加展览
Attending an Exhibition

Notes

1. In short, you can get all the information about the products, customers and competitors under one roof.
   总之，你可以在一个地方得到所有的有关产品、客户和竞争对手的信息。

2. The following are just a few of the wide array of benefits when attending these kinds of events.
   以下仅是参加这类活动诸多好处中的一小部分。

3. This is beneficial in the sense that it can help increase the public awareness with regards to your product offerings and services.
   它可以提高公众对贵公司的产品和服务的认识，这是很有益处的。

4. It also creates favorable impression among the attendees, in knowing that you are personally visiting them at the event.
   知道您亲自去拜访他们，会给与会者留下良好的印象。

5. You can also be more competitive in the sense that you can increase your sales leads.
   由此，不但可以增加您的销售机会，还会增加您的竞争力。

Answer the following questions.

1. What are the benefits of attending trade shows and exhibitions? Make a list.
2. What is the main purpose of attending exhibitions or trade shows?

Decide whether the following statements are True or False based on the above passage.

1. The benefits of attending trade shows and exhibitions are numerous. (　　)
2. If you are planning to promote your products or services, attending an exhibition is an unwise decision. (　　)
3. You will realize a very few resources and opportunities in a single event. (　　)
4. Attending a trade show will increase your exposure to your respective industry. (　　)
5. You can get many indirect contacts by just attending an exhibition or trade show. (　　)
6. Through the exhibitions, you can increase your client-base which will enhance your sales. (　　)

Exercises

1. Match the words on the left with their proper meaning on the right.

(1) attend   a. someone who supports something

(2) exhibition   b. something shown to the public

(3) apply   c. confirm the truth of

(4) verify   d. put into service

(5) display   e. a collection of things

(6) sponsor   f. be present at

(7) payment   g. a formal event performed on a special occasion

(8) receipt   h. amounting to a large indefinite number

(9) numerous   i. the act of receiving

(10) ceremony   j. a sum of money paid

2. Read the following statements, and fill in the blank spaces with the appropriate words contained in the word box.

opportunity   target   exhibitions   strategies   products   newspapers

(1) The changing nature of consumer's tastes and preferences has meant that companies have had to change their advertising _____.

(2) Marketers no longer solely focus on traditional advertising methods such as television and _____.

(3) Exhibitions and trade shows are now the commonly-used ways of promoting _____ and services in cost-effective manner.

(4) Companies and marketers can interact with their _____ consumers via exhibitions and trade shows.

(5) Exhibitors can obtain an increased number of clients, customers, sales and contacts by attending _____.

(6) Usually, all exhibitors are situated in the same area. This will provide you with the _____ to analyze your competitor's strategies and products.

3. Translate the following sentences into English.

(1) 我打算参加第八届东北亚博览会。

(2) 但是我们对参展程序一无所知。

(3) 如果需要特别的帮助,尽管联系我们。

(4) 选择这样一个展会真是明智之举。

4. Role play.

(1) You are a receptionist at an Auto Show. Mr. James is a first-time visitor and he wants to know something about the Auto Show.

(2) You are a receptionist at an International Agricultural Products Trade Fair. Mr. White is a company VIP representative. He is going to attend the seminar of the International Agricultural Products Trade Fair, but he doesn't have any information about the seminar.

 Practical Training Project 实训项目

Perform research on the Internet, concerning an exhibition that is of interest to your company. Prepare a 10-minute presentation introducing the show and recommending why your company should exhibit at this event.

Unit 6

Booth Decorating
展 位 装 饰

Unit 6

展位装饰
Booth Decorating

Learning Objectives 学习目标

After learning this unit, you will be able to:
★ Design an attractive booth display.
★ Know how to decorate a booth.
★ Improve your skills to attract potential customers' attention.
★ Master the useful expressions and sentences.

Background Information 背景知识

装饰与设计一个独特而醒目的展位对于展会的成功及企业参展目标的实现都是至关重要的。具有高度视觉冲击力的展台将吸引与会者对参展商的业务的关注，使人过目不忘，给观众带来良好的第一印象，有助于企业的形象宣传和产品宣传。此外，展位的位置、大小、标志、宣传材料和工作人员的个性，都是展会成功举办的主要要素。

Lead-in 导入活动

Trade shows bring awareness of your company to clients, buyers and vendors. Creating an eye-catching, noticeable and effective trade show booth is essential to the success of the event.

【拓展视频】

A high-impact display will draw attendees to your business, generate that interest in which your company is offering, and leave them with a memorable impression. An attractive booth may generate incomes for you after the show. Booth location, size, signage, handouts and staff personality all contribute to an effective and successful trade show.

Warm-up 热身活动

Match and Discuss

Directions: Match the pictures in the left column with the activities in the right column, and discuss with your partner to determine how much you understand about booth decorating activities.

1.    A. attracting customers' attention

2.    B. decorating a booth

3.    C. designing a booth

4.    D. building a booth

Unit 6

展 位 装 饰
Booth Decorating

Basic Reading 基础阅读

Tips on Decorating a Trade Show Booth

Great products may sell themselves, but not if they don't get noticed. At trade shows, each exhibitor is trying to out-do the others to attract attention to their booths. Creating a booth display that is easy to see and find is a large part of the battle. Once people see your booth, they must feel comfortable, and be able to see and gather information easily and quickly.

※ Height

Create a height in your booth. Some companies make the mistake of laying everything out flat on a table. Even tabletop displays must have a height. Purchasing tabletop magazine racks, business card holders, and sign holders that stand up make it easier for customers to see your information. Never expect people to lean over your table to view anything in the display. Even if you are limited to a tabletop display, you can still use pop-up tabletop units. These units are easy to assemble and make it easy for visitors to see your information. Height and pop-ups also make it easier for large groups of people to see your exhibits at the same time.

※ Signs and Banners

Never assume people will find you; announce your presence with easy-to-see signs. Hang signs up high with banners and large pictures that are easier to see from far away. You can attract people to your booth from a distance by hanging colorful pictures and easy-to-read signs with big colorful letters. Red letters are easy to read from far away.

※ Color and Comfort

A booth should feel comfortable to your potential customers. If people feel comfortable, they are more likely to spend more time on the booth, and this increases your chance of making a sale.

Instead of having your visitors stand on a cold floor, bring a warm rug to walk on. Use warm general lighting to keep the booth cheerful, but use directional lighting to highlight display items or sections that you want people to pay attention to.

Color is important. Trade show booths often use cool blue, such as gray and white that will look very professional. To stand out, and give a more comfortable feel, consider using warmer tones and include red and yellow to get attention and brighten the space in your display.

Vocabulary

battle	['bætl]	n.	战役
gather	['gæðə(r)]	v.	聚集
height	[haɪt]	n.	高度
flat	[flæt]	adj.	扁平的；单调的
rack	[ræk]	n.	行李架
lean	[liːn]	v.	倾斜
assemble	[ə'sembl]	v.	装配
assume	[ə'sjuːm]	v.	假定
announce	[ə'naʊns]	v.	宣布
rug	[rʌg]	n.	小地毯
section	['sekʃn]	n.	部门；地区
tone	[təʊn]	n.	语气；音调

Notes

1. Great products may sell themselves, but not if they don't get noticed.
   酒香不怕巷子深，但是如果好的产品没有得到关注，那么情况就不同了。

2. Some companies make the mistake of laying everything out flat on a table.
   一些公司会犯这样的错误：把所有的东西都平放在桌面上。

3. Height and pop-ups also make it easier for large groups of people to see your exhibits at the same time.
   高度和弹出窗口会更容易让一大群人在同一时间看到你的展品。

4. You can attract people to your booth from a distance by hanging colorful pictures and

easy-to-read signs with big colorful letters.

你可以悬挂彩色图片和有大号彩色字母的醒目的牌匾，从远距离就可以吸引人们到你的展台。

5. Instead of having your visitors stand on a cold floor, bring a warm rug to walk on.

不要让参观者站在冰冷的地板上，而是让参观者走在温暖的地毯上。

6. To stand out, and give a more comfortable feel, consider using warmer tones and including red and yellow to get attention and brighten the space in your display.

要想脱颖而出，并使人感觉更舒适，可以考虑使用温暖的色调，包括红色和黄色，以引起别人的注意，并且使你的展示空间更明亮。

Discuss the following question with your partner.

What are the tips on booth decoration? Make a list first, and then give a brief summary.

【拓展术语】

 ## Situational Dialogues 情景对话

Dialogue 1

Alice is an exhibition organizer; Mr. Liu is an exhibitor. They are having a discussion about booth building, booth decorating and requirements for safety & security concerns.

A=Alice   L=Mr. Liu

A: Hi, Mr. Liu, nice to see you again.

L: Hi, Alice, nice to see you too. I would like to tell you some good news. What you did for us last year impressed our customers so much that we'd like to cooperate with you again this year.

A: Really, I'm happy to hear that.

L: Now, I'd like to talk with you about booth building, booth decorating and particularly our safety & security concerns.

A: OK. Our staff can help you with all your requirements.

L: Great. We'll have some special requirements for the booth design. Also, our exhibits are of great value.

A: I see. We have well-trained safety and security personnel, and facilities to guarantee the safety of your valuables.

L: We'll need round-the-clock safety services for the exhibits including security guards' patrolling and camera monitoring.

A: I can arrange all for you. Is there anything else?

L: Yes, we'd like to have some models help show off our latest designs.

A: No problem. How many models do you want?

L: Altogether, we will need twenty models.

A: OK, I'll see to it. Do you think it is necessary to prepare some small gifts for the visitors?

L: Yes! We've made some artificial crystal key chains for our visitors. I wonder if you could help design some unique gift bags.

A: Of course. But I'd like to see the shape and size of the key chains firstly. And how many gift bags will you need?

L: 100. I'll soon let you see the style of our key chains for your reference.

A: Good. What you need to do is to download an exhibition application form from our website and fax it to me after you complete it.

L: OK, thanks so much.

Vocabulary

security	[sɪˈkjʊərəti]	n.	安全
affair	[əˈfeə(r)]	n.	事情；事务
requirement	[rɪˈkwaɪəmənt]	n.	要求
personal	[ˈpɜːsənl]	adj.	个人的
facility	[fəˈsɪləti]	n.	设施
patrol	[pəˈtrəʊl]	n.	巡逻
camera	[ˈkæmərə]	n.	照相机
monitor	[ˈmɒnɪtə(r)]	n.	监视器
artificial	[ˌɑːtɪˈfɪʃl]	adj.	人造的
crystal	[ˈkrɪstl]	n.	水晶
unique	[juˈniːk]	adj.	独特的
reference	[ˈrefrəns]	n.	参考
application	[ˌæplɪˈkeɪʃən]	n.	申请

Notes

1. What you did for us last year impressed our customers so much that we'd like to cooperate with you again this year.
   因为去年你们的服务给我们的客户留下了深刻的印象，所以今年我们想与你们再度合作。

2. safety & security personnel 安保人员
   For example: We have well-trained safety & security personnel, and facilities to guarantee

the safety of all the valuables.

例如：我们有专门培训的保安人员和安全设施，可以确保贵重物品的安全。

3. round-the-clock 昼夜，24 小时

For example: We'll need round-the-clock safety services for the exhibits, including security guards' patrolling, and camera monitoring.

例如：我们需要对展品进行 24 小时的保安服务，包括保安巡逻和电子监控。

4. show off 卖弄，炫耀；展示

For example: We'd like to have some models help show off our latest designs.

例如：我们需要一些模特为我们展示最新设计的产品。

5. I'll see to it.

我来处理。

6. Exhibition Application Form 参展申请表

【拓展音频】

Dialogue 2

In the following dialogue, Aimee, who is from a fashion company, and Mr. Li, a booth designer, are having a talk on designing a distinctive booth, and use giveaways to attract new customers.

A=Aimee   L=Mr. Li

A: Good morning, Mr.Li!

L: Good morning, Aimee！Are you here for your booth design?

A: Yes, of course! As you know, our company is not experienced in attending such an important international trade show, so I am here to request your valuable suggestions.

L: I am certainly pleased to offer my helpful suggestions.

A: It is so kind of you! Firstly, what theme do you think we should adopt for our booth?

L: The theme of your booth should focus your company's target customers.

A: We are a fashion company, and our target customers are young and fashionable people.

L: I see. So the theme of your booth should help your company achieve the modern image.

A: Then what should we do to build such a booth that is full of fashionable features?

L: You need to get furniture such as desks, chairs, shelves, and include imitation fashion models that will look unique and kind of cool.

A: Good idea. What else can we do to make our booth more attractive?

L: I suggest you use some bright colors, and good-quality materials to build the booth.

　　　　If possible, you can also consider a special lighting effect in your booth.

A: OK, we will definitely give our best efforts to do so.

L: One more thing. Flowers and soft music may help you to attract more customers.

A: All right. Thanks a lot. Your suggestions are really valuable for us.

L: My pleasure. I am looking forward to visiting your fashionable booth.

Vocabulary

distinctive	[dɪˈstɪŋktɪv]	adj.	有特色的
giveaway	[ˈɡɪvəweɪ]	n.	免费样品
theme	[θiːm]	n.	主题
achieve	[əˈtʃiːv]	v.	达到；完成
image	[ˈɪmɪdʒ]	n.	影像；肖像；偶像
furniture	[ˈfɜːnɪtʃə(r)]	n.	家具；设备
shelf	[ʃelf]	n.	架子；搁板
imitation	[ˌɪmɪˈteɪʃn]	n.	仿制品

Notes

1. I am certainly pleased to offer my helpful suggestions.
   如果我的建议能给您一些帮助的话，我会很高兴的。

2. It is so kind of you.
   你真是太好了。

3. The theme of your booth should focus your company's target cutomers.
   您的展台主题应聚焦贵公司的目标客户。

4. The theme of your booth should help your company achieve the modern image.
   您的展台主题应该呈现贵公司现代感的一面。

5. that is to say 也就是说

6. I am looking forward to visiting your fashionable booth.
   我期待参观贵公司充满时尚感的展台。

【拓展音频】

📖 Useful Sentences 常用口语

1. I'd like to talk with you about booth building concerns.
   我想和您谈谈展台搭建事宜。

2. What products would you like to display?
   您想展示什么样的产品呢？

3. How would you like us to decorate your booth?
   您希望我们如何装饰您的展台?

4. We want our booth to look attractive.
   我们希望展台富有吸引力。

5. What kind of booth do you suggest?
   你建议搭建什么类型的展台呢?

6. Any special requirements for the decoration?
   您对于装饰有什么特殊要求吗?

7. We want every booth to be decorated with our company's logo.
   我希望每个展台都有我们公司的标志。

8. Do you think it is necessary to prepare some small gift's for the visitors?
   你认为有必要准备一些小礼物给宾客吗?

9. What theme do you think we should adopt for our booth?
   你认为我们应该采用什么样的展台主题?

10. The theme of your booth should focus your company's target cutomers.
    您的展台主题应聚焦贵公司的目标客户。

11. What else can we do to make our booth more noticeable?
    怎么做才能使我们的展台更引人注意呢?

12. I suggest you use some materials with bright colors, and a special lighting effect is also very important.
    我建议采用一些亮色的材料,特殊的灯光效果也十分重要。

 Further Reading 拓展阅读

Design Tips for a Trade Show Booth

When your company exhibits at a trade show or conference, the face of your company or organization is the artwork you have created for your booth. You have about three seconds to catch an attendee's attention. Choosing the right blend of imagery, text and color can mean the differences between someone stopping to visit your booth or walking over to your competitor's booth.

※ **Know Your Target Audience**

When planning your design, think firstly about what would be appealing to your target audience. Consider what images, words, colors or messages will mean the most to the people that matter the most. If you are selling a product, for example, try to find a photograph of one of your customers using that product. If you can't find an actual customer, look for stock photography that matches the profile of your typical customer. Don't substitute a model of a young teen, if in fact your company targets middle-aged women. Also, your message should reflect your company's main selling point, product or mission in that languages your customers will understand. Keep the wording simple, with large, and bold headlines. Too much text will detract from the overall strategy. You'll also want to include a "call-to-action" phrase incorporating such language as "to order, call…" or "for more information, ask your booth representative". Use any phrases that encourage your potential customer to take the next step in the buying cycle.

※ **Know Your Company's Branding**

Do not forget the identity of your company when designing your booth graphics. Your company has invested money, time and resources to create a specific branding. Make sure your color scheme is consistent with your company's color palette. You should use complimentary colors that match the brand. If there are specific images or catch phrases that always appear in company messaging, be sure to include those features as well. You might also consider how your company is portrayed in promotional campaigns. If your direct mail, e-mail and signage all reflect a common theme, then you'll want to replicate the branding in your booth graphics.

※ **Know Your Medium**

One of the most important elements of booth design is sizing and placement. The elements must "pop", and they must stand out at a distance. Consider using a singular image, or a singular grouping of images, for impact, and make sure the most important elements of the imagery are located at the eye level or just below or above. The same approach should be applied to text. A single, and bold headline is best, and it is important to place the text at the top of your display. The same concept applies to your company's URL, logo or name. When possible, also consider using lighting with an eye toward enhancing your design. Avoid too many images or too much text. Remember, you have three seconds to impress.

Unit 6

展位装饰
Booth Decorating

Vocabulary

blend	[blend]	n.	混合
profile	['prəʊfaɪl]	n.	侧面；轮廓
mission	['mɪʃn]	n.	使命
bold	[bəʊld]	adj.	大胆的
detract	[dɪ'trækt]	v.	使分心
incorporate	[ɪn'kɔːpəreɪt]	adj.	合并的
identity	[aɪ'dentəti]	n.	身份
graphic	['græfɪk]	adj.	形象的；图表的
scheme	[skiːm]	n.	计划
consistent	[kən'sɪstənt]	adj.	一致的
palette	['pælət]	n.	调色板
complimentary	[ˌkɒmplɪ'mentri]	adj.	称赞的
portray	[pɔː'treɪ]	v.	描绘；扮演
replicate	['replɪkeɪt]	n.	复制品
approach	[ə'prəʊtʃ]	n.	方法

Notes

1. When your company exhibits at a trade show or conference, the face of your company or organization is the artwork you have created for your booth.
   当贵公司在贸易展或会议上参展的时候，贵公司或组织的面貌就是您为您的展位所创造的一件艺术品。

2. Don't substitute a model of a young teen, if in fact your company targets middle-aged women.
   如果贵公司的目标是中年妇女，那就不要用一个青少年做模特。

3. Also, your message should reflect your company's main selling point, product or mission in language your customers will understand.
   另外，贵公司应该用您的客户能够理解的语言介绍贵公司的主要卖点、产品或使命。

4. If there are specific images or catch phrases that always appear in company messaging, be sure to include those features as well.
   如果公司的信息中总是出现特定的图像或文字，请务必保留这些信息。

Answer the following questions.

1. What are the design tips for a trade show booth? Make a list firstly, and then give a brief summary.

2. What are the possible factors for booth designing?

3. Can you explain the standard for a good booth design?

Decide if the following statements are True or False based on the above passage.

1. When your company exhibits at a trade show, the face of your company is the artwork you have created for your booth. ( )

2. You have lots of time to catch an attendee's attention. ( )

3. Choosing the right blend of imagery, text and color can mean the differences between someone stopping to visit your booth or walking over to your competitor's booth. ( )

4. One of the most important elements of booth design is lighting effectiveness. ( )

5. You should ignore the identity of your company when designing your booth graphics. ( )

6. The designing elements must "pop", and they must stand out at a distance. ( )

Exercises

1. Match the words on the left with their proper meaning on the right.

(1) gather   a. an abstract part of something

(2) height   b. furnishings that make a room ready for occupancy

(3) tone   c. the single one of its kind

(4) announce   d. someone who supervises (an examination)

(5) assume   e. equipment for taking photographs

(6) camera   f. take to be the case or to be true

(7) monitor   g. make known

(8) unique   h. the quality of a person's voice

(9) furniture   i. the distance from the base of something to the top

(10) element   j. get together

2. Read the following statements and fill in the blank spaces with the appropriate words enclosed in the word box.

draw   allow   questions   interesting   space   advance

(1) If you are scheduled to exhibit at a fair, plan your booth design well in _____.

(2) You may purchase a stand-alone booth, or a "turn-key" booth—a blank _____ to which you add your own flair and signage.

(3) Booth design is a strong marketing tool: an _____ design should bring a constant flow of customers to your table.

(4) Place two posters on either side of the front of your booth. The purpose of these posters is to _____ the browser to your table. If he is interested, he will then likely move in closer to read more.

(5) If the viewer is still interested after reading your poster, he will likely grab for a flyer and start asking you _____.

(6) If your booth structure does not _____ you to comfortably hang two posters, purchase an easel to place next to your booth.

3. Translate the following sentences into English.

(1) 把一切东西都平放在桌子上是有些参展公司常犯的错误。

(2) 我期待参观你们充满时尚感的展台。

(3) 展台主题主要由公司的定位来决定。

(4) 空间是展台设计中必须要考虑的重要因素之一。

4. Role play.

Make up a dialogue based on the following situation.

Mr. White and Ms. Zhang are from an automobile company who are going to attend an auto show. They are discussing how to make their booth more distinctive, as compared to other booths.

Practical Training Project 实训项目

The opening speech is one of the most important aspects of successful business dealings. Imitate the opening address of the general secretary of Changchun International Auto Exposition and deliver an exposition opening address to the exhibitors and visitors.

Unit 7

Reception at the Booth
展 台 接 待

Unit 7

展台接待
Reception at the Booth

Learning Objectives 学习目标

After learning this unit, you will be able to:
★ Know how to introduce a new product to the clients.
★ Attract more buyers to your booth.
★ Receive clients appropriately at the booth.
★ Build a friendly business relationship at the first contact.

Background Information 背景知识

给客户留下良好的第一印象，并在和客户打交道的过程中赢得客户的好感、信任和尊重，进而为生意洽谈创造有利的条件，是客户接待工作的重中之重。因此，接待人员需要结合企业自身的产品及服务，分析预测客户的各种潜在需求（如对产品信息方面的需求、对展台环境、展品布置及对服务态度和服务设施的需求等），并努力满足客户的需求，取得客户的信赖与合作，实现双赢的目标。

Lead-in 导入活动

【拓展视频】

Trade shows represent great opportunities for promoting your business. At an effective show, you can achieve the goal of informing people of your products and services in order to make your brand name more visible. Ideally, you may achieve your ultimate goal, and sell your products into a defined market.

How can you achieve your ultimate goal? The secret is: for the clients, the decision to buy is often initiated with the first impression of service. So, learning how to receive clients or how to help the clients accept your products is the key to a successful trade show display.

Warm-up 热身活动

Match and Discuss

Directions: Match the pictures in the left column with the activities in the right column, and discuss with your partner to determine how much you understand about receiving clients.

1.  A. entertaining clients with business dinners

2.  B. introducing new products to the clients

3.  C. attracting more clients to the booth

4.  D. greeting clients at a booth

Unit 7
展 台 接 待
Reception at the Booth

Basic Reading 基础阅读

Necessary Staff for an Effective Trade Show Exhibit

An eye-catching and high-impact trade show exhibit can draw visitors to your booth. Pre-marketing and event participation will also attract people who are interested in what you have to offer.

Yet, it is mandatory that your booth staff create a meaningful dialogue with your visitors and identify who are high prospects for further follow-up. The impression your team members make while working the booth, will determine how effective they are at qualifying and generating viable leads.

Your visitors will not judge you and your product, merely through the beauty of your trade show display. Rather they will consider your staff's behavior and appearance as the key to their interest level in your product.

According to authors Jay Levinson, Mark Smith and Orvel Wilson in their book *Guerrilla Trade Show Selling*, the following staff's behaviors annoy booth visitors and inhibits sales effectiveness, based on surveys they conducted.

Top Nine Things That Drive Visitors Nuts:

1. Being ignored.
2. A staff that doesn't know the products.
3. Staff members eating in the exhibit area.
4. Being interrupted.
5. Hands in pockets.
6. Being kept around when they're ready to leave.
7. Chewing gum.
8. Continuous throat-clearing.
9. Bad breath.

While not doing these behaviors seems obvious, they tend to happen to some degree at every event. It is therefore strongly suggested that you don't only invest in your exhibit display without planning to devote the time in training your staff to achieve proper professional behaviors, and achieve top performances.

Vocabulary

mandatory	['mændətəri]	adj.	义务的
prospect	['prɒspekt]	n.	预期
qualify	['kwɒlɪfaɪ]	v.	有资格
generate	['dʒenəreɪt]	v.	发生
viable	['vaɪəbl]	adj.	可行的；能养活的
appearance	[ə'pɪərəns]	n.	外观
guerrilla	[gə'rɪlə]	n.	游击战
annoy	[ə'nɔɪ]	v.	骚扰；惹恼
inhibit	[ɪn'hɪbɪt]	v.	抑制；禁止
ignore	[ɪg'nɔː(r)]	v.	忽视
interrupt	[ˌɪntə'rʌpt]	v.	打断

Notes

1. Pre-marketing and event participation will also attract people who are interested in what you have to offer.

   前期的市场营销和每场活动将吸引那些对您的产品感兴趣的人。

2. Rather they will consider your staff's behavior and appearance as the key to their interest level in your product.

   相反，他们会认为您的员工的外表和行为是他们对您产品感兴趣的关键。

3. While not doing these behaviors seems obvious, they tend to happen to some degree at every event.

Unit 7
展台接待
Reception at the Booth

虽然不做这些行为似乎是显而易见的，但它们往往在某种程度上会在每一个展会中发生。

4. It is therefore strongly suggested that you don't only invest in your exhibit display without planning to devote the time in training your staff to achieve proper professional behaviors, and achieve top performances.

因此，强烈建议您不要只在展示的展品上进行投资，而没有考虑投入时间培训员工，以确保他们有正确的职业行为和最佳表现。

Discuss the following question with your partner.

The behaviors that are not allowed by the trade show staff.

【拓展术语】

 Situational Dialogues 情景对话

Dialogue 1

Mr. Jiang, a member of the marketing staff of the Dragon Electronics Co. Ltd., is receiving a customer, Mr. White, at a trade show. He is introducing a new digital voice recorder pen to Mr. White.

J=Mr. Jiang　　　W=Mr. White

J: Good afternoon, Sir! Welcome to our booth.

W: Good afternoon!

J: If you don't mind, could you please tell me what products you are interested in?

W: This new product looks good. Is it a digital voice recorder pen?

J: Yes. This is indeed a new type pen that our company highly recommends.

W: What type of new functions does it have?

J: It is not only a great voice recorder, but also a telephone recorder and cell phone recorder. And its MP3 function allows you to listen to your pleasing music anywhere you desire. It is compact and portable.

W: Good. It seems quite convenient, especially in a business meeting.

J: You are exactly right. This new type pen is actually designed for business use, and can save both time and space by using such a multi-functional device.

W: But I am worried that this kind of multi-functional device will have more problems than the simple devices.

J: Don't worry about that. This type is different from other multi-functional devices. It has been carefully tested. You can completely trust its quality.

93

W: Amazing! If it is really as good as you have just said, then I will purchase this new product for our company.

J: You can talk to our technician to get the further details. And, you can contact us either by e-mails or phone calls.

W: Ok. I will think about it.

J: Thank you, and would you please leave us your contact information?

W: Of course. Here is my name card.

J: Thank you.

Vocabulary

digital	['dɪdʒɪtl]	*adj.*	数字的
recommend	[ˌrekə'mend]	*v.*	推荐
function	['fʌŋkʃn]	*n.*	功能
compact	[kəm'pækt]	*adj.*	紧凑的；简洁的
portable	['pɔːtəbl]	*adj.*	轻便的
device	[dɪ'vaɪs]	*n.*	装置
purchase	['pɜːtʃəs]	*n.*	购买
technician	[tek'nɪʃn]	*n.*	技师；技术人员

Notes

1. This new product looks good.
   这个新产品看起来不错。

2. highly recommend 强力推荐

   For example: This is indeed a new type pen that our company highly recommends.
   例如：这确实是我公司极力推荐的一种新型钢笔。

3. What type of new functions does it have?
   它有哪些新功能？

4. It seems quite convenient.
   看起来非常方便。

5. You are exactly right.
   您说得太对了。

6. design for 为……设计

   For example: This new type pen is actually designed for business meeting use.
   例如：这款新笔实际上就是专门为商务会议设计的。

Unit 7

展台接待
Reception at the Booth

【拓展音频】

7. multi-functional device 多功能设备
8. It can save both time and space by using such a multi-functional device.
   使用这种多功能设备既省时间，又节约空间。

Dialogue 2

Miss Zhou is a customer. She is inquiring about the products of Mr. Wang's company.

Z=Miss Zhou   W=Mr. Wang

W: Good afternoon, Miss.

Z: Good afternoon, Sir.

W: Welcome to our display.

Z: May I ask what are your main products?

W: Multimedia players. They are designed to be used in classrooms.

Z: May I have a look at the samples?

W: Sure. This is the brochure of our newest products.

Z: What is the advantage of your company products?

W: Our company is renowned for multimedia players. They are now highly ranked nationally.

Z: How?

W: Our company has a first-class management group, and skilled technicians. Our quality is guaranteed, and sold at competitive prices.

Z: How can I contact you?

W: This is our company's name card, and my business card. Please contact us whenever needed.

Z: Thank you.

W: Meanwhile, we wish to offer you a catalog containing our newest products for your reference.

Z: Fine, thank you.

W: You're welcome.

Vocabulary

multimedia	[ˌmʌltiˈmiːdiə]	n.	多媒体
brochure	[ˈbrəʊʃə(r)]	n.	手册
advantage	[ədˈvɑːntɪdʒ]	n.	优势
renowned	[rɪˈnaʊnd]	adj.	著名的
competitive	[kəmˈpetətɪv]	adj.	竞争的

Notes

1. May I ask what are your main products?
   请问你们的主打产品是什么?

2. multimedia players 多媒体播放器

3. May I have a look at the samples?
   我可以看看样品吗?

4. This is the brochure of our newest products.
   这是我们公司最新产品的介绍手册。

5. be renowned for 因……而著名;以……著称

   For example: Our company is renowned for multimedia players. They are now highly ranked nationally.
   例如:我们公司以生产多媒体播放器著称,在行业内处于领先地位。

6. first class 一流的

   For example: Our company has a first-class management group, and skilled technicians.
   例如:我们公司有一流的管理队伍和技术人员。

7. meanwhile 同时;其间

   For example: Meanwhile, we wish to offer you a catalog containing our newest products for your reference.
   例如:同时,我们送您一本最新系列产品的目录,以供您参考。

【拓展音频】

Useful Sentences 常用口语

1. Could you recommend a new product?
   你能介绍一款新产品吗?

2. I wonder if you could give me some information about your company.
   不知您能否告诉我一些贵公司的信息。

3. If you don't mind, could you tell me what products you are interested in?
   如果您不介意,可否告诉我您对什么产品感兴趣?

4. This is indeed a new type pen that our company highly recommends.
   这确实是我公司极力推荐的一种新型钢笔。

5. What kinds of new function does it have?
   它有哪些新功能呢?

6. Could you please leave your contact number so that we can provide you with our latest information?
   为了能更好地为您服务,您可以留下您的联系方式吗?

7. These are the samples of our company's products.
   这是我们公司产品的样品。

8. May I ask what are your main products?
   请问，你们的主打产品是什么？

9. May I have a look at the samples?
   可以看看样品吗？

10. This is the brochure of our newest products.
    这是我们公司最新产品的介绍手册。

11. What is the advantage of your company products?
    贵公司的产品优势在哪儿？

12. Our company has a first-class management group, and skilled technicians. Our quality is guaranteed, and sold at competitive prices.
    我们公司有一流的管理阶层和技术人员，质量有保证且价格适中。

Further Reading 拓展阅读

A relationship begins the moment a client comes to your booth. The ways we look, walk, act and talk are important factors as to how people relate to us. How we talk and behave will show whether we really care about the clients' views and feelings. That will leave a deep impression on our clients, which may decide whether we can do business with them successfully or not. No matter who we are, salespeople, receptionists or managers, we know some basic and important things to improve our opportunity to succeed is necessary. To start with, we should always wear a smile on our face or look pleasant. A friendly smile is an important way to help potential clients relax. It can affect clients and make our booth warm and inviting. Some people think that it is convenient to serve our clients when we stand in the center of the booth. However, that's not true. Stand off to the side, near the front corner of the exhibit. To create a more inviting appearance, don't directly face the aisle and stare at attendees. Moreover, focus your attention on our clients and what they talk about. We should try our best to be interested and listen carefully. People tend to like people who like them. Treat others as you would like to be treated. As we know, clothes make the man or woman. So please iron your clothes, cut your hair and act like professionals. Our posture is an expression of our confidence and personality. So we should stand upright and make our clients feel that we're confident and energetic. Don't be slouchy. Finally, please allow plenty of open space for our clients to browse. We should stand at least 3 feet from the displays or equipment. Be an observer, and not a guard. Allow prospects to approach the displays without your interference. A too small space may make clients feel uncomfortable and even claustrophobic.

Vocabulary

receptionist	[rɪˈsepʃənɪst]	n.	接待员
appearance	[əˈpɪərəns]	n.	外貌
aisle	[aɪl]	n.	通道；侧廊
stare	[steə(r)]	n.	凝视；注视
slouchy	[ˈslaʊtʃi]	adj.	懒散的；没精打采的
browse	[braʊz]	v.	浏览
equipment	[ɪˈkwɪpmənt]	n.	设备

Notes

1. The ways we look, walk, act and talk are important factors as to how people relate to us.
   我们观察、走路、行为及谈话的方式，是我们与人交往的重要因素。

2. No matter who we are, salespeople, receptionists or managers, we know some basic and important things to improve our opportunity to succeed is necessary.
   无论销售员、接待员还是经理，了解一些能提高成功几率的基本的、重要的知识是必要的。

3. People tend to like people who like them.
   人们往往喜欢那些喜欢他们的人。

4. As we know, clothes make the man or woman.
   众所周知，人靠衣装马靠鞍。

5. So we should stand upright and make our clients feel that we're confident and energetic.
   因此，我们应该站姿挺拔，使我们的客户觉得我们是有信心和充满活力的。

6. A too small space may make clients feel uncomfortable and even claustrophobic.
   过小的空间可能会令客户感到不适，甚至会产生压抑的感觉。

Unit 7
展台接待
Reception at the Booth

Answer the following questions.

1. What is the main topic of this passage?
2. What can be the best title of this passage?

Decide whether the following statements are True or False based on the above passage.

1. Always wear a smile on your face or look pleasant. ( )
2. Stand in the center of the exhibit, hold a small piece of paper in your hands and stare at clients, saying "Welcome to our booth and enjoy our exhibition". ( )
3. Show your respect to clients and be interested in clients' views and questions. ( )
4. Dress professionally and be confident. ( )
5. Put more tables in the showroom and show more products to your clients. A small space will make your clients feel your booth is full and abundant. ( )
6. Stand in the booth with your arms folded. ( )

Exercises

1. Match the words on the left with their proper meaning on the right.

(1) appearance   a. a fixed look with eyes open wide
(2) ignore   b. reading superficially or at random
(3) survey   c. to make better
(4) digital   d. showing reason or sound judgments
(5) access   e. a small book usually having a paper cover
(6) brochure   f. reach or gain access to
(7) reasonable   g. displaying numbers rather than scale positions
(8) improve   h. the act of looking or seeing or observing
(9) browse   i. fail to notice
(10) stare   j. outward or visible aspect of a person or thing

2. Read the following statements, and fill in the blank spaces with the appropriate words contained in the word box.

attention   combination   clients   introduce   business   right

(1) The first step to get more business _____ is to make a list of your existing business partners.

(2) You can ask your existing business partners to _____ you to companies and individuals they work with.

(3) In some cases existing vendors or customers of your partners could be interested in doing _____ with you, too.

(4) Instead of trying to sell to everybody, center your _____ on those people who have already expressed an interest in what you're offering.

(5) Getting new clients is a _____ of a sequence of steps that work together to get the end result.

(6) It's so important that you do all the right steps in the _____ order to get the results.

3. Translate the following sentences into English.

(1) 欢迎您浏览我们公司的网站。

(2) 贵公司的拳头产品是什么？

(3) 这是我们公司最新产品的介绍手册。

(4) 现在是我们新产品的推广期。

4. Role play.

Make up a dialogue based on the following situations.

(1) Suppose you are a business representative of a computer company. Introduce your products to a potential customer at an exhibition.

(2) Suppose you are promoting a new type of shampoo at an exhibition. While meeting your regular customer, Mr. White, have a conversation with him.

Practical Training Project 实训项目

Mr. Brake is the general manager of the Dragon Electronics Co., Ltd. in Shenyang. You are a sales manager of Changchun Hongda Company, which specializes in manufacturing digital voice recorders. Mr. Brake and you meet for the first time at this show.

Task 1

Make a dialogue which takes place at your booth.

* You two get to know each other.

* You successfully present your products and get Mr. Brake interested in them.

* You talk about the possibility of the business.

* You invite Mr. Brake to have dinner at China Hotel and he agrees.

Unit 7 展台接待 Reception at the Booth

Task 2

Devise a conversation which takes place at dinner.

* You recommend a product.
* You get to know more about his company.
* You both are more optimistic about the possibility of further business relationship.
* Mr. Brake will stay in Changchun for 3 more days for sightseeing after this show.
* You recommend some scenic spots, which greatly arouse his interest.

Unit 8

Sales Presentation
销售展示

Unit 8 销售展示 Sales Presentation

Learning Objectives 学习目标

After learning this unit, you will be able to:
★ Make professional presentations to individuals and companies.
★ Attract clients with an effective product presentation.
★ Communicate effectively with clients.
★ Master useful expressions for a presentation.

Background Information 背景知识

销售演示(Sales Presentation)是一种现场销售模式，即由有经验的销售人员现场操作，展示实际产品特色功效及如何使用，从而使消费者产生购买欲，进而达到销售的目的。演示过程是顾客了解与体验产品的过程，也是销售人员诉求商品利益的最佳时机。恰当时机的选择、良好氛围的营造、销售辅助物的恰当运用、有效的交流与沟通等，这些都是演示过程中需要特别注意的。

Lead-in 导入活动

【拓展视频】

During a trade fair, there is usually a sales presentation to promote your products or services. This is an effective way to attract a visitor's attention. For a successful sales presentation, the following strategies will help you:

◇ Make the presentation relevant to your potential client or customer.
◇ Create a connection between your products and the prospect's needs; know your potential customer's needs.
◇ Get to the point; be concise.
◇ Be animated and use showmanship.
◇ Pay special attention to your physiological signals, and use a physical demonstration; be energetic.
◇ Believe in your product; be confident.

Warm-up 热身活动

Match and Discuss

Directions: Please look at the following pictures and read the descriptions of different types of sales presentation. Match each picture with the right description respectively.

1.

A. With the high cost of travel, teleconference sales presentation is a good way to reduce costs.

2.

B. Webinar sales presentations are conducted via the Internet. Webinar lets those, who choose to view the sales presentation, watch it on their computer.

Unit 8
销 售 展 示
Sales Presentation

3.    C. Team sales presentations are those performed by more than one person.

4.    D. Seminar sales presentations are held in an auditorium or a large venue.

 Basic Reading 基础阅读

Conducting a sales presentation can resemble a show and tell. But, there's much more to it than that. Strategy is a large part of the process. The following sales presentation tips will help you to make a successful sales presentation.

There are lots of techniques that can attract a potential customer's attention. You also need to evaluate your audience's responses so that you can take further steps toward your ultimate goal, sales! Your presentation, either for group audience or for an individual, should be as brief as possible while summarizing the fundamental points of your business. Keep your audience interested, and remember not to make your presentation long-lasting.

A typical newspaper article is a good example of how to construct your presentation. Touch upon all the essential points you wish to make, using illustrations as needed to highlight those key points of your presentation.

As you are emphasizing the key points, maintain eye contact and possibly ask questions in order to interact with your audience. For example, "Are you aware of similar products elsewhere?" You need to master the techniques of involving your audience in your presentation, and be flexible through modifying your dialogue by observing their body languages.

If people arrive late for your presentation, ensure that they feel included in your discussions.

After a reasonable period of time, it's helpful for you to ask direct questions to determine whether you should continue, or move to conclude the presentation.

Vocabulary

conduct	[kənˈdʌkt]	v.	进行
resemble	[rɪˈzembl]	v.	类似
technique	[tekˈniːk]	n.	技巧
fundamental	[ˌfʌndəˈmentl]	adj.	根本的
indication	[ˌɪndɪˈkeɪʃn]	n.	指示
compose	[kəmˈpəʊz]	v.	构成；写作
essential	[ɪˈsenʃl]	adj.	本质的
illustration	[ˌɪləˈstreɪʃn]	n.	插图
emphasize	[ˈemfəsaɪz]	v.	强调
interact	[ˌɪntərˈækt]	v.	互相影响
conclude	[[kənˈkluːd]	v.	结束

Notes

1. Conducting a sales presentation can resemble a show and tell.
   进行销售展示类似于一个表演和介绍。
2. Your presentation, either for group audience or for an individual, should be as brief as possible while summarizing the fundamental points of your business.
   当你在陈述业务基本要点时，无论是面对团体观众还是个人，你的展示都应尽量简短。

3. Touch upon all the essential points you wish to make, and use illustrations, as needed, to highlight those key points of your presentation.
   涉及所有你希望说明的要点，并且可以根据需要使用插图，突出关键点。
4. As you are emphasizing the key points, maintain eye contact and possibly ask questions in order to interact with your audience.
   当你强调重点时，应保持目光交流，并且问一些问题，以便与你的听众互动。
5. You need to master the techniques of involving your audience in your presentation, and be flexible through modifying your dialogue by observing their body languages.
   你需要掌握能让你的听众全神贯注于你的展示的技巧，并且通过观察他们的肢体语言灵活地改正你的谈话。

Discuss the following question with your partner.

In your opinion, what are the most effective tips for producing a good sales presentation? Make an outline of your thoughts, and then give a brief summary.

【拓展术语】

Situational Dialogues 情景对话

Dialogue 1

Mr. Harmer, a sales manager, is presenting his company's products to a potential customer.

H= Mr. Harmer   C= customer

H: Hello, good morning. My name is Harmer. I am the sales manager with Huada Garment Company Limited. May I have a few minutes of time to alert you to a few of our newest products?

C: Ok.

H: These are our latest designed pants samples.

C: What makes them better than other pants on the market?

H: There are a number of factors. They are more durable than others in the marketplace.

C: Why does it take longer to wear out than the others?

H: We use a carefully selected, high-quality, and tightly woven yarn in the fabric to make all of our pants.

C: Could you leave these samples with us?

H: How long do you want to keep them?

C: About two weeks.

H: OK, no problem. You can keep them for the requested time period.

C: Thank you very much.

Vocabulary

garment	[ˈɡɑːmənt]	n.	服装
alert	[əˈlɜːt]	v.	使意识到
durable	[ˈdjʊərəbl]	adj.	耐用的
marketplace	[ˈmɑːkɪtpleɪs]	n.	市场
yarn	[jɑːn]	n.	纱线
fabric	[ˈfæbrɪk]	n.	织物；构造

Notes

1. These are our latest designed pants samples.
   这是我们最新设计的裤装样品。

2. What makes them better than other pants on the market?
   什么使它们优于市场上的其他裤子？

3. They are more durable than others in the marketplace.
   它们比市场上的同类产品更耐用。

4. wear out 穿破；磨损；用坏

   For example: Why does it take longer to wear out than the others?
   例如：为什么它比其他产品耐用呢？

5. We use a carefully selected, high-quality, and tightly woven yarn in the fabric to make all of our pants.
   我们用精心挑选、高品质、密实的纱线做我们所有的裤子。

【拓展音频】

Dialogue 2

R=representative   C=customer

R: Hello sir, welcome to our display.

C: Hello madam.

R: I am the business representative for our company. Could I introduce our products to you now?

C: Ok.

R: This way, please. These are a few samples of our products.

C: What are your main products?

Unit 8

Sales Presentation
销售展示

R: These are the main ones of our company. We specialize in all types of kitchen products. Please have a look.

C: OK. Which kitchen appliances do you manufacture?

R: Dishwashers, refrigerators, toasters, coffee systems, microwave-ovens, etc.

C: A very complete line of products!

R: You are right. Our products are well-known at home and abroad, and mainly exported to Asia, Africa and South America.

C: Do you enjoy a good market share?

R: Yes we do, by producing quality products, with a reasonable price, while concentrating on the needs of our consumers.

C: I'm interested in your dishwashers.

R: We have large, medium and small-sized dishwashers. Our latest dishwasher has many new functions. Please have a look.

C: Very good. Do you still have other models?

R: Yes, but due to the limited space, we can't demonstrate all of our models. However, you may browse our website. This way, please.

(After 20 minutes)

C: Your website is quite good. Are all the products listed in the website?

R: Yes. If you want to know more about our products, or have any questions, please contact us. This is my business card. May I have your contact number?

C: Sure. Here is my business card. I will keep in touch with you. Thank you for your presentation. Goodbye.

R: My pleasure. See you.

Vocabulary

kitchen	[ˈkɪtʃɪn]	n.	厨房
appliance	[əˈplaɪəns]	n.	器具
refrigerator	[rɪˈfrɪdʒəreɪtə(r)]	n.	冰箱
toaster	[ˈtəʊstə(r)]	n.	烤面包器；烤箱
microwave	[ˈmaɪkrəweɪv]	n.	微波
function	[ˈfʌŋkʃn]	n.	功能
demonstrate	[ˈdemənstreɪt]	v.	展示
website	[ˈwebsaɪt]	n.	网站

Notes

1. What are your main products?

贵公司的主要产品是什么？

2. specialize in 专攻；专门经营；擅长

   For example: We specialize in all types of kitchen products.
   例如：我们专业生产厨房用品。

3. A very complete line of products!
   一条非常完整的产品线！

4. Our products are known at home and abroad, and mainly exported to Asia, Africa and South America.
   我们的产品驰名中外，主要出口亚洲、非洲和南美洲。

5. You may browse our website.
   您可以浏览我们公司的网站。

【拓展音频】

Useful Sentences 常用口语

1. Many thanks for coming.
   多谢您的光临。

2. I would like to express my appreciation.
   我谨表示我的感谢。

3. That is most thoughtful of you.
   您想得真周到。

4. At your service.
   愿意为您效劳。

5. Can I see how it works?
   我能看看它是怎样操作的吗？

6. Why do you think these products are popular with young people?
   你为什么认为这些产品会受到年轻人的欢迎？

7. How about your quality control?
   贵公司的质量管理如何呢？

8. Our products are of the highest quality.
   我们的产品质量是最好的。

9. Our demand is greater than our supply.
   我们的产品供不应求。

10. Our products can help you to significantly increase market share, with great returns.
    我们的产品能够帮助您大幅度提高市场占有率，您将从中极大获益。

11. You cannot find a better product on the market.
    您在市场上找不到更好的产品了。

12. Our products have the best value for money, so there is a stable consumer group.
    我们的产品的性价比很高，所以有稳定的消费群。

Further Reading 拓展阅读

Creating a Powerful Sales Presentation

by Kelley Robertson

The quality of your sales demonstration will often determine whether a prospect buys from you or from one of your competitors. Here are seven demonstration tips that will help you create a sales presentation that will motivate buyers.

1. Make the relevant demonstration.

One of the most common mistakes people make is to use a generic presentation. They say the same thing in every demonstration with the expectation that something in their demonstration will hopefully appeal to the prospective customers. Do not become a victim to this approach. Discussion of your product or service must be adapted to each person; modify it to include specific points that are unique to a particular customer. If you use a PowerPoint, place the company's logo on your slides and describe how the key slides relate to their situations. Show exactly how your product or service solves their specific problems.

2. Create a connection between your product/service and the prospect.

In a demonstration to a prospective client, I prepared a sample of the product they would eventually use in their program. After a preliminary discussion, I provided a sample of the product and placed it in the client's hands. This was the same product that his team would be using – instead of telling him about the product; it was now in his hands. He could then see exactly what the finished product would look like and examine it in detail. He was able to ask questions and see how his team would use it in their environment.

Also, remember to discuss the benefits of your products, not the features. Tell your customers what they will get by using your product versus your competitors'.

3. Get to the point.

Today's business people are far too busy to listen to long-winded discussions. Know what your key points are and learn how to make them quickly. I remember talking to a sales person who rambled at great length about his product. After viewing his product and learning how much it would cost I was prepared to move ahead with my purchase. Unfortunately, he continued talking and he almost talked himself out of the sale. Make sure you know what key points you want to discuss and practice verbalizing them before you meet with your prospect.

4. Be animated.

The majority of sales demonstrations I have heard has been boring and unimaginative. If you really want to stand out from the crowd make sure you demonstrate enthusiasm and energy. Use voice effectively and vary your modulation. A common mistake was made when people talk about a product they are very familiar with is to speak in a monotone – causing the other person to quickly lose interest in your demonstration.

5. Use showmanship.

In *The Sales Advantage*, an example is given of a vending sales person laying a heavy sheet of paper on the floor, saying, "If I could show you how a space could make you some money, would you be interested?"

6. Use a physical demonstration.

A friend of mine sells sales training seminars. He often uses the whiteboard or flipchart in the prospect's boardroom during his demonstration. Instead of telling his clients what he will do, he stands up and delivers a short demonstration. He writes down facts and figures, draws pictures, and records certain comments and statements from the discussion. This approach never fails to help his prospect make a decision.

7. Believe in your product/service.

Without doubt, this is the most critical component of any demonstrations. When you discuss solutions, do you become more animated and energetic? Does your voice display excitement? Do your body languages exhibit your enthusiasm? If not, you need to change your approach. After all, if you can't get excited about your product, how can you expect your customers to become motivated enough to buy?

Vocabulary

motivate	['məʊtɪveɪt]	v.	使有动机
generic	[dʒə'nerɪk]	adj.	一般的
victim	['vɪktɪm]	n.	牺牲品
approach	[ə'prəʊtʃ]	n.	方法

Unit 8
销售展示 Sales Presentation

modify	['mɒdɪfaɪ]	v.	修改
preliminary	[prɪ'lɪmɪnəri]	adj.	初步的
versus	['vɜːsəs]	prep.	与……相对
ramble	['ræmbl]	v.	漫谈
verbalizing	['vɜːbəlaɪzɪŋ]	v.	以言语表述
animated	['ænɪmeɪtɪd]	adj.	活泼的
majority	[mə'dʒɒrəti]	n.	多数
enthusiasm	[ɪn'θjuːziæzəm]	n.	热情
modulation	[ˌmɒdjʊ'leɪʃən]	n.	调整
monotone	['mɒnətəʊn]	n.	单音调
showmanship	['ʃəʊmənʃɪp]	n.	表演技巧
vend	[vend]	v.	出售
component	[kəm'pəʊnənt]	n.	成分

Notes

1. The quality of your sales demonstration will often determine whether a prospect buys from you or from one of your competitors.
   你展示的产品的质量往往会决定一个潜在的客户是从你那里还是从你的竞争对手那里购买产品。

2. They say the same thing in every demonstration and hope that something in their demonstration will appeal to the prospective customers.
   在每一次展示中，他们都重复同样的话，并且希望他们展示的某些产品会吸引潜在的客户。

3. Today's business people are far too busy to listen to long-winded discussions.
   现在的商务人士太忙了，没有时间听长篇大论。

4. A friend of mine sells sales training seminars. He often uses the whiteboard or flipchart in the prospect's boardroom during his demonstration.
   我的一位朋友从事销售培训研讨会的经营活动，在展示时他经常使用潜在客户会议室中的白板或活动挂图。

Answer the following questions.

1. What are the guidelines to create a powerful sales presentation? Please give a brief explanation.

2. What is the most important part in creating a successful sales presentation?

Decide whether the following statements are True or False based on the above passage.

1. In a sales presentation, we should always use a nonspecific power point file. (　)
2. Company logo is totally unnecessary in a demonstration. (　)
3. A sample of the product may help you in a presentation. (　)
4. A monotonous voice is usually acceptable in a sales presentation. (　)
5. Before we meet with our prospect, we should know what key points we want to discuss and practice verbalizing those thoughts. (　)
6. It is very important that you have faith in your products for any presentation. (　)

Exercises

1. Match the words on the left with their proper meaning on the right.

   (1) essential   a. ask for
   (2) durable   b. pick out
   (3) kitchen   c. anything that contributes causally to a result
   (4) function   d. make different
   (5) period   e. sell or offer for sale from place to place
   (6) vend   f. an amount of time
   (7) modify   g. what something is used for
   (8) factor   h. a room equipped for preparing meals
   (9) select   i. existing for a long time
   (10) request   j. absolutely necessary

2. Read the following statements, and fill in the blank spaces with the appropriate words contained in the word box.

   | slides   result   presentation   person   customer   advertisements |

   (1) A sales presentation is an advertisement delivered in _____ to the customer.
   (2) The sole purpose of a sales presentation is to make the _____ buy your product.
   (3) In consumer world, _____ are extensively used either in TV or radio or magazines/paper or Internet.
   (4) But in business to business world, advertising through conventional media does not work, so companies developed a set of _____ –which contain certain messages to the customer.
   (5) And this set of slides is conventionally called as "sales _____".

(6) In most business to business sales, the first meeting will not _____ in closing the deal or winning the order. So the objective for the very first presentation must be set accordingly.

3. Translate the following sentences into English.

(1) 这是我们最新设计的女装样品。

(2) 我们的产品驰名中外，远销亚洲、非洲和南美洲。

(3) 在同样的价格下，我们提供的产品质量更高。

(4) 我们的产品有着良好的性价比，所以有稳定的消费群。

4. Role play.

Work in pairs or more. Try to do a short play according to the following instruction.

Suppose you are at a convention booth, and introducing your products to several visitors. There is a dialogue, back and forth. Play out the conversation as you think it will happen.

Practical Training Project 实训项目

You represent an electronic products corporation, based in Changchun, and you have handled the export of electronic products for many years. Knowing that your company has been in this line of business for many years, a businessman from America comes to see if it is possible to enter into business relations with you. You should present your products to him in detail and provide him with the new products catalogues. The following are some of the aspects you may cover when doing your presentation.

※ Identify or clarify your unique selling points of your main products.

※ Highlight Sales Achievements, Sales Increases, Market Share Growth and Sales Rankings of your products, both domestic and abroad.

※ Emphasize The Warranty or Guarantee on your product.

※ Promise the after-sales services.

Unit 9

Business Negotiation
商务谈判

Unit 9 商务谈判 Business Negotiation

Learning Objectives 学习目标

After learning this unit, you'll be able to:

★ Know how to ask for information about disagreement on price, and getting a more favorable price by negotiating.

★ Know how to enhance your skills at negotiating deals.

★ Know how to develop new markets at a lower price.

★ Master some useful expressions and sentences.

Background Information 背景知识

商务谈判（Business Negotiation），是买卖双方为了促成交易而进行的活动，或是为了解决买卖双方的争端，并取得各自的经济利益的一种方法和手段。

商务谈判活动应遵循以下原则：①双赢原则；②平等原则；③合法原则；④时效性原则；⑤最低目标原则。

Lead-in 导入活动

【拓展视频】

For a good salesman and negotiator, there are several principles you should follow.

◇ Don't believe anything you see and hear.
◇ Don't offer your bottom line earlier in the negotiation.
◇ Sell and negotiate simultaneously.
◇ Be patient.

Warm-up 热身活动

Match and Discuss

Directions: Match the pictures in the left column with the business etiquette activities in the right column, and discuss with your partner to determine how much you understand about etiquette in business negotiation.

1. 　　　A. farewell etiquette

2. 　　　B. etiquette for signing agreement

3. 　　　C. business dinner etiquette

4. 　　　D. greeting etiquette

Basic Reading 基础阅读

Price has become one of the most sensitive and important factors in today's business negotiations. Before buyers place an order for products, they need a price, the terms for the sale, the delivery time, etc. Buyers will always want to purchase the best commodities at reasonable prices, while the sellers wish to make the highest possible profit. In order to get the best value for the money, buyers must have a clear understanding of all relevant information. Good salespeople are typically good negotiators. But so are the good buyers. Negotiation is a process that can be learned. By following the rules outlined here, and with adequate practice, you can perfect your skills at negotiating deals, in which everyone wins.

※ **Prepare in Advance**

Information is powerful. Obtain as much information as possible beforehand to make sure you understand the value of what you are negotiating.

※ **Ask Questions**

Clarify information you do not understand. Determine both the implicit and explicit needs of your counterpart.

※ **Listen**

When you do a good job listening, you not only gain new ideas for creating win-win outcomes but also make your counterpart feel appreciated and valued.

※ **Be Honest, Fair, Cooperative and Friendly**

※ **Never Accept the First Offer**

The other party will often make an offer that he or she thinks you will refuse just to see how firm you are on key issues.

※ **Be Prepared to Walk Away**

The bottom line here is: If you are not willing to walk away from the negotiation, you are not emotionally able to say to yourself "That's OK, I will find another more acceptable situation tomorrow". You will lose. I guarantee it!

Vocabulary

sensitive	['sensətɪv]	adj.	敏感的
term	[tɜːm]	n.	期限；条款
delivery	[dɪ'lɪvəri]	n.	递送
purchase	['pɜːtʃəs]	v.	购买
commodity	[kə'mɒdəti]	n.	商品
reasonable	['riːznəbl]	adj.	合理的
profit	['prɒfɪt]	n.	利润；利益
relevant	['reləvənt]	adj.	有关的
adequate	['ædɪkwət]	adj.	充足的
obtain	[əb'teɪn]	v.	获得
clarify	['klærəfaɪ]	v.	阐明
implicit	[ɪm'plɪsɪt]	adj.	含蓄的
explicit	[ɪk'splɪsɪt]	adj.	清楚的
counterpart	['kaʊntəpɑːt]	n.	对应的人或物
cooperative	[kəʊ'ɒpərətɪv]	adj.	合作的
guarantee	[ˌgærən'tiː]	v.	保证；担保

Notes

1. Before buyers place an order for products, they need a price, the terms for the sale, the delivery time, etc.
   在买家下订单订购产品之前，他们需要价格、销售条款及交货时间等方面的信息。

2. By following the rules outlined here, and with adequate practice, you can perfect your skills at negotiating deals, in which everyone wins.
   遵循这些原则，再加以充分实践，你就可以完善自身的谈判技能，在谈判中实现双赢。

3. When you do a good job listening, you not only gain new ideas for creating win-win outcomes but also make your counterpart feel appreciated and valued.
   当你仔细聆听时，你不但可以获得创造双赢结果的新想法，而且会让你的对手感到被欣赏和受到重视。

4. The other party will often make an offer that he or she thinks you will refuse just to see how firm you are on key issues.
   对方往往会提出一个他/她认为你会拒绝的报价，就是为了看你在关键问题上有多么坚定。

Unit 9

商 务 谈 判
Business Negotiation

Discuss the following questions with your partner.

1. What is the main topic of this passage?
2. What can be the best title of this passage ?
3. How to perfect your skills at negotiating deals in which everyone wins?

【拓展术语】

Situational Dialogues 情景对话

Dialogue 1

Mrs. Jenny Keats, the purchasing manager, is interested in the pure cotton commodities offered by Mr. Wang's company. Now she is discussing the price at Mr. Wang's booth, expecting that he will give her a better discount.

J=Mrs. Jenny Keats   W=Mr. Wang

J: I've been assigned to negotiate with you about cotton commodities.

W: May I know what particular items you are interested in at this time?

J: I'm interested in your pure cotton commodities. I've seen the exhibits and studied your catalogs. And I think they will find a ready market in America.

W: Great. Here are our latest price sheets. Would you like to have a look?

J: Your price is too high! It will be difficult for us to make any sales.

W: But you should take the quality into consideration. Our products are superior in quality, while moderate in price, and are sure to be salable in your marketplace.

J: I'm afraid it is impossible for us to accept your offer. The difference between your offer and the price we are willing to pay, is too wide.

W: You know the price of cotton has gone up since last year. Our price is relatively favorable.

J: It's unwise for either of us to stick to one's own price. How about meeting each other halfway, and making a further concession, so that business can be concluded?

W: If your order is large enough, we will consider reducing our price by 5 percent.

Vocabulary

assign	[əˈsaɪn]	v.	分配；指派
particular	[pəˈtɪkjələ(r)]	adj.	特别的
item	[ˈaɪtəm]	n.	条款；项目
catalog	[ˈkætəlɒg]	n.	目录

121

superior	[suːˈpɪərɪə(r)]	adj.	优秀的；出众的
relatively	[ˈrelətɪvli]	adv.	相对地
stick	[stɪk]	v.	坚持；粘住
halfway	[ˌhɑːfˈweɪ]	a.	中途的
reduce	[rɪˈdjuːs]	v.	减少；缩小

Notes

1. May I know what particular items you are interested in at this time?
   您这次对哪类产品感兴趣？

2. Your price is too high!
   你们的价格太高了！

3. take into consideration 考虑到，顾及；把……考虑进去
   For example: You should take the quality into consideration.
   例如：您应该考虑到质量问题。

4. The difference between your offer and the price we are willing to pay, is too wide.
   我们的心理价位与你方报价之间的差距太大。

5. stick to 坚持，忠于，信守；紧跟，紧随；粘贴在……上
   For example: It's unwise for either of us to stick to one's own price.
   例如：我们双方都坚持自己的价格是不明智的。

6. how about 如何，怎么样
   For example: How about meeting each other halfway? And in that way, business can be concluded.
   例如：能不能双方都各让一步，这样生意就有可能成交。

【拓展音频】

Dialogue 2

Mrs. Li is satisfied with the first-class quality products offered by Mr. Huang's company. Now she is discussing the further cooperation with Mr. Huang.

L=Mrs. Li   H= Mr. Huang

H: I can promise you that, if you buy our products, you will be getting good quality.

L: I've looked at your units, and I am very happy with them. Your goods are all above standard quality.

H: We spend a lot of money ensuring that our quality is better.

L: Well, we're really interested in placing an order. We can start the negotiation as soon as you want.

H: That's great. I'm glad we will be able to do business together. I'll have some quotes ready for you very soon.

L: Fine. Also, would you mind if I asked to see an assessor's report of your products? I may have more questions concerning your quality analysis.

Vocabulary

promise	['prɒmɪs]	v.	允诺
standard	['stændəd]	n.	标准
quality	['kwɒləti]	n.	质量
quote	[kwəʊt]	n.	引用；报价
assessor	[ə'sesə(r)]	n.	评审员
analysis	[ə'næləsɪs]	n.	分析

Notes

1. ensure 确保，确定

   For example: We spend a lot of money ensuring that our quality is better.
   例如：我们投入了大量的资金来确保质量一流。

2. We can start the negotiation as soon as you want.
   我们可以尽快开始谈判。

3. place an order 下订单

   For example: We're really interested in placing an order.
   例如：我方真的很愿意订货。

4. would you mind if

   后面接从句时，从句中的谓语动词常为过去式，用来表示委婉的语气，译为：你介意……吗？

   For example: Would you mind if I asked to see an assessor's report of your products?
   例如：您不介意我要求看一下贵方产品的检验报告吧？

5. I may have more questions concerning your quality analysis.
   对你们的质量分析我可能还有更多的问题。

【拓展音频】

 Useful Sentences 常用口语

1. I'd like to get the ball rolling by talking about the price.
   言归正传，我们谈谈价格。

2. I'd be happy to answer any questions you may have.
   我愿意解答您的任何疑问。

3. Your products have very good quality. But I am a little worried about the prices you are asking for.
   贵公司的产品质量好。但我对您的报价有顾虑。
4. We'd like a guarantee of future business, not just a promise.
   我们是要未来合作的保证而不仅仅是承诺。
5. If you can guarantee that on paper, I think we can discuss this further.
   如果您能做书面保证，我想我们可以进一步讨论。
6. I'd say that we are interested in these products. Could you give us some ideas of your prices?
   我想说我们对这些产品比较感兴趣。可不可以让我们了解一下价格？
7. Here are our price lists.
   这些是我们的价目表。
8. I'm sure you realize that the costs of new materials have recently gone up considerably.
   但是我相信您也知道，最近材料的价格直线飙升。
9. Compared with the prices offered by other firms, our prices are very competitive.
   相比其他公司的开价，我们的价格算是很有竞争力的了。
10. I must tell you that your prices are higher than some quotations we have received from other firms.
    我必须告诉您，你们的价格比我们收到的其他公司的报价要高。
11. If we are to place an order with you, I think a discount of about 10% would be necessary.
    如果要我们订购的话，我认为10%的折扣还差不多。
12. Your counter-offer is too low and unreasonable.
    你的还价太低，而且不合理。

 Further Reading 拓展阅读

Tips on Managing the Sales Negotiation Process

How you handle the sales negotiation process will determine whether you close the sale or not, and how profitable that sale will be. If you can refer to the following key points, you will be able to manage the sales negotiation process.

※ **Don't Believe Anything You See and Hear**

Part of a good salesperson's skill is to learn to read people and situations very quickly. However, when it gets down to negotiating, you have to take everything you see and hear with a grain of salt. Buyers are good negotiators, and thus they are good actors. You may be the only person who has what she needs, but everything she does and says, from body languages to the words she uses, will be designed to lead you to believe that unless she gets an extra 10% off, she's going with the competitors. Be skeptical. Be suspicious. Test, probe, and see what happens.

※ Don't Offer Your Bottom Line Early in the Negotiation

How many times have you been asked to "give me your best price"? Have you ever given your best price only to discover that the buyer still wanted more? You have to play the game. It's expected. If you could drop your price by 10%, start out with 0%, or 2%, or 4%. Leave yourself room to negotiate. Who knows - you may get the sale at a 2% discounted offer. You might have to go all the way to 10%, but often you won't. A little stubbornness pays big dividends.

※ Get Something in Return for Your Added Value

What if you discover that the buyer wants to be able to track his expenditures for your products or services in a way that is far more detailed and complex than that is standard for your industry? What if your account tracking system is set up in a way that you can provide that information at essentially no cost for you? Often the salesperson's overwhelming temptation is to jump in and say, "Oh, we can do that. That's no problem." Before you do agree, think about your options. You could throw it in the part of the package and try to build good will. Or you could take a deep breath and try something like, "That's a difficult problem that will require some efforts on our part, but it's doable". In the second case, without committing, you've told the buyer that it is impossible. You may not be able to get him to pay extra for it, but you may be able to use it as a bargaining chip in resisting price concessions. Which way you choose to go will depend on who your customer is on the situation. However, you do have options.

※ Sell and Negotiate Simultaneously

Think of selling and negotiating as two sides of the same coin. Sometimes one side faces up, and sometimes the other side, but they are always both there. This is particularly true in your earliest contacts with the buyer. The face the buyer sees is that of a salesperson demonstrating features and benefits. The hidden face is that of a negotiator probing and seeking out information that may be invaluable later should issues like price, terms, quality, delivery, etc. have to be negotiated.

※ Be Patient

Finally, and most importantly, be patient. Sales is a high energy, and fast moving business. Patience is one commodity that is in a relatively short supply, but if you're impatient in a negotiation, you'll lose your shirt. If I'm negotiating with you and I know that you're impatient, I will hold out just a little longer, no matter how desperate I am to make a deal with you. As long as I know you're in a hurry, I'll wait. So be patient. Take the time that you need, don't rush to give in, don't show your anxiety, stay cool and don't panic. Negotiation is a process, and a game. Use the process and play the game. You'll be astonished at the differences that it makes!

Vocabulary

handle	['hændl]	v.	处理
skeptical	['skeptɪkl]	adj.	怀疑的
suspicious	[sə'spɪʃəs]	adj.	可疑的
probe	[prəʊb]	v.	调查；探测
reduction	[rɪ'dʌkʃn]	n.	减少
stubbornness	['stʌbənnɪs]	n.	倔强
dividend	['dɪvɪdend]	n.	股息；奖金
expenditure	[ɪk'spendɪtʃə(r)]	n.	花费
overwhelming	[ˌəʊvə'welmɪŋ]	adj.	压倒性的
temptation	[temp'teɪʃn]	n.	引诱
doable	['duːəbl]	adj.	可做的
bargain	['bɑːgən]	v.	讨价还价
concession	[kən'seʃn]	n.	让步
simultaneously	[ˌsɪml'teɪniəsli]	adv.	同时地
invaluable	[ɪn'væljuəbl]	adj.	非常贵重的
commodity	[kə'mɒdəti]	n.	商品
relatively	['relətɪvli]	adv.	相对地
desperate	['despərət]	adj.	令人绝望的
anxiety	[æŋ'zaɪəti]	n.	焦虑
panic	['pænɪk]	v.	十分惊慌
astonished	[ə'stɒnɪʃt]	adj.	吃惊的

Notes

1. How you handle the sales negotiation process will determine whether you close the sale or not, and how profitable that sale will be.

Unit 9
商务谈判
Business Negotiation

你如何处理销售谈判过程将决定你能否完成销售,以及销售的利润如何。

2. However, when it gets down to negotiating, you have to take everything you see and hear with a grain of salt.
然而,当谈判进入正轨时,你必须对你所看到和听到的一切持谨慎态度。

3. You may be the only person who has what she needs, but everything she does and says, from body languages to the words she uses, will be designed to lead you to believe that unless she gets an extra 10% off, she's going with the competitor.
你也许是唯一一个拥有她所需要产品的人,但她的一言一行,都故意让你以为如果你不给她再打10%的折扣,她就会跑去与你的竞争对手合作。

4. Have you ever given your best price only to discover that the buyer still wanted more?
是否在你已给出最优惠价格后,却发现买方仍然想要更多优惠?

5. The hidden face is that of a negotiator probing and seeking out information that may be invaluable later should issues like price, terms, quality, delivery, etc. have to be negotiated.
如果价格、条款、质量和交货等需要协商,鲜为人知的一面便是谈判者正在调查和寻找今后可能会非常有价值的信息。

Answer the following questions.

1. What guidelines or tips will help you succeed in the sales negotiation process? Make a list.
2. What are your thoughts concerning the following statement? "Don't Believe Anything You See and Hear."
3. What benefits can be achieved by being patient during a business negotiation?

Decide whether the following statements are True or False based on the above passage.

1. How you handle the sales negotiation process will determine whether you close the sale or not. (   )
2. All of a good salesperson's skill is to learn to read people and situations very quickly. (   )
3. Buyers are good negotiators, and thus they are good actors. (   )
4. We should always think of selling and negotiating as two sides of the same coin. (   )
5. Sales is a high energy and fast moving business. (   )
6. Negotiation is a game and destination. (   )

Exercises

1. Match the words on the left with their proper meaning on the right.

(1) obtain a. an overwhelming feeling of fear and anxiety
(2) bottom b. enduring without protest or complaint
(3) stick c. an amount of something available for use
(4) reduce d. the act of reducing the selling price of merchandises
(5) promise e. make available or accessible, provide or furnish
(6) offer f. grounds for feeling hopeful about the future
(7) discount g. cut down on
(8) supply h. a small thin branch of a tree
(9) patient i. the lower side of anything
(10) panic j. come into possession of

2. Read the following statements, and fill in the blank spaces with the appropriate words contained in the word box.

| both | negotiating | parties | lie | contact | out |

(1) Body language will always reveal the truth even when the words being spoken are a _____.

(2) Watch their body languages and, in particular, their eyes. If they can't give you eye _____ when they're demanding something, it will almost always mean they don't believe their request is reasonable.

(3) We use the selling process as a way of finding _____ what the customer is expecting to pay or accept from you.

(4) The higher level of trust between the two _____, is the less need there is for tactics.

(5) If you're negotiating with a person in whom you have little trust, you'll be forced to use more _____ tactics.

(6) Don't start any negotiation unless _____ parties are in agreement about what is going to be negotiated.

3. Translate the following sentences into English.

(1) 价格已经成为商务谈判中最敏感和最重要的因素之一。
(2) 如果我们双方都各让一步，生意就可能成交。
(3) 如果你们对这些条款和条件满意的话，那就请下订单吧。
(4) 很高兴我们特装展位价格谈判在最后一轮终于达成一致。

4. Role play.

(1) Make up a dialogue based on the following situation.

Ms. Smith, a representative of ABC Import & Export Co, Ltd, has tested the samples of digital cameras from BCD Electronic Products Corp. before the China Import and Export Fair. Now she is at the BCD Electronic Products Corporation booth, expecting a good price quotation. You are the representative of BCD Electronic Products Corp.

(2) Student A:

• You are the buyer, Mr. James.

• Talk with Ms. Li about the prices of the silk skirts.

• Ask for 10% off.

• Make a concession in the end.

Student B:

• You are the exhibitor, Ms. Li.

• Talk with Mr. James concerning the prices of the silk skirts.

• Insist on 5% off only.

• Try to offer other incentives such as giveaways to close the deal.

 Practical Training Project 实训项目

Work in groups of 6 students. 3 students act as the Sellers while the other 3 act as the Buyers. Each group conducts a comprehensive negotiation covering the following aspects: price, quantity, payment, packing, insurance, etc. Be sure to use the terms, sentence patterns and negotiation skills mentioned in this unit. After rehearsal, each group will perform the whole negotiation process in class.

Unit 10

Insurance
保 险

Unit 10 保险 Insurance

Learning Objectives 学习目标

After learning this unit, you will be able to:
★ Make a list of event risks.
★ Describe the basic types of insurance.
★ Deal with insurance issues.
★ Master the useful expressions for insurance.

Background Information 背景知识

众所周知，展品是供展示的样品，特别是国际展，展品在去程和回程运输途中由于周期长、环节多，极易损坏，从而丧失其展示和使用价值，给参展商带来不可估量的经济和信誉损失。有效规避风险的最好办法就是保险。因此，我们有必要对相关知识有所了解，并在此基础上选择合适的险别。

Lead-in 导入活动

【拓展案例】

Whether your exhibition is a local or a global trade show, it is not immune from the risks which can affect any events, such as: terrorism, strikes, adverse weather conditions, damage to property (your own property or property that belongs to the venue), reduced attendance due to some unforeseen events, etc.

In some occasions, you may have had difficult situations, and exhibition disasters may eventually happen to you. Therefore, be ready with the right insurance. You'll not only be able to ensure your ability to deal with any unfortunate situations, but you'll also have the peace of mind that you will have a better chance of being able to return to display your wares as quickly as possible.

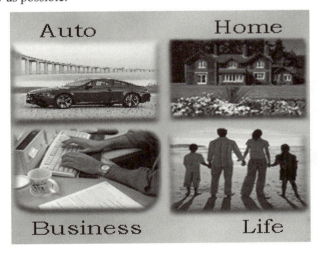

Warm-up 热身活动

Match and Discuss

Directions: Please look at the following pictures and read the descriptions of various sorts of insurance. Match each picture with the right description respectively.

1.    A. WA/WPA: With Average or With Particular Average

2.    B. All Risks

3.    C. War or Terrorist Risk

4.    D. FPA: Free from Particular Average

Unit
保　　险
Insurance
10

Basic Reading 基础阅读

The Effects of Insurance

Insurance can have various effects on society through the way that it changes who bears the cost of losses and damage. On the one hand it can increase fraud, but it can also help societies and individuals prepare for catastrophes, and lessen the effects of catastrophes on both households and societies.

Insurance can influence the probability of losses through moral hazard, insurance fraud, and preventive steps by the insurance company. Insurance scholars have typically used morale hazard to refer to the increased loss due to unintentional carelessness and moral hazard to refer to increased risk due to intentional carelessness or indifference. Insurers attempt to address carelessness through inspections, policy provisions requiring certain types of maintenance, and possible discounts for loss mitigation efforts. While in theory insurers could encourage investment in loss reduction, and some commentators have argued that in practice insurers had historically not aggressively pursued loss control measures-particularly to prevent disaster losses such as hurricanes-because of concerns over rate reductions and legal battles. However, since about 1996 insurers began to take a more active role in loss mitigation, such as building codes.

Vocabulary

fraud	[frɔːd]	n.	欺骗；诡计
catastrophe	[kəˈtæstrəfi]	n.	大灾难；大祸
mitigation	[ˌmɪtɪˈgeɪʃn]	n.	缓和
influence	[ˈɪnfluəns]	v.	影响
probability	[ˌprɒbəˈbɪləti]	n.	可能性
moral	[ˈmɒrəl]	adj.	道德的
hazard	[ˈhæzəd]	n.	危险；冒险
preventive	[prɪˈventɪv]	adj.	预防的
indifference	[ɪnˈdɪfrəns]	n.	漠不关心
insurer	[ɪnˈʃʊərə(r)]	n.	承保人
inspection	[ɪnˈspekʃn]	n.	检查
maintenance	[ˈmeɪntənəns]	n.	保持
reduction	[rɪˈdʌkʃn]	n.	减少
commentator	[ˈkɒmənteɪtə(r)]	n.	评论员
aggressively	[əˈgresɪvli]	adv.	积极地
hurricane	[ˈhʌrɪkən]	n.	飓风

Notes

1. Insurance can influence the probability of losses through moral hazard, insurance fraud, and preventive steps by the insurance company.
   道德风险、保险欺诈及保险公司的防范措施是否得当都会影响损失发生的概率。

2. Insurance scholars have typically used morale hazard to refer to the increased loss due to unintentional carelessness and moral hazard to refer to increased risk due to intentional carelessness or indifference.
   保险专家通常所用的心理风险是指（投保人）非故意疏忽或麻痹大意而导致的损失增加的风险，道德风险是指（投保人）故意疏忽或故意不重视而造成的损失增加的风险。

3. While in theory insurers could encourage investment in loss reduction, and some commentators have argued that in practice insurers had historically not aggressively pursued loss control measures - particularly to prevent disaster losses such as hurricanes - because of concerns over rate reductions and legal battles.
   理论上讲，保险公司可能会鼓励（投保人）在减少损失方面的投入，但一些评论家认为，实际上保险公司在历史上并没有积极地寻求控制损失的措施——尤其是防范飓风等灾害带来的损失——因为保险公司担心投保率下降，害怕陷入法律纷争。

Unit 10 保险 Insurance

【拓展术语】

Discuss the following question with your partner.

What are the positive & negative effects of insurance?

Situational Dialogues 情景对话

Dialogue 1

Mr. Brown, a sales manager of an exhibition company, is inquiring about insurance issues with Miss Wang, a staff member of an insurance company.

B=Mr. Brown   W=Miss Wang

B: May I ask you a few questions about insurance?

W: Yes.

B: We recently gave a CIF concerning a Dalian price for some iron ores. What insurance rate do you suggest we should acquire?

W: Well, obviously you won't want All Risks coverage.

B: Why not?

W: Because the iron ores are not delicate goods, and they most probably won't be damaged on the voyage. FPA will be good enough.

B: Then am I right in understanding that FPA does not cover partial loss for the nature of particular average?

W: That's right. On the other hand, a WPA policy covers you against partial loss in all cases.

B: Are there any other clauses in marine policies?

W: Oh, lots of them! For example, War Risks, TPND and SRCC.

B: Well, thank you very much for all that information. Could you give me a quotation for my consignment now?

W: Are you going to make an offer today?

B: Yes, our customer is in an urgent need of the iron ores.

W: OK. I'll immediately get the rate for you.

B: Thank you.

Vocabulary

insurance   [ɪnˈʃʊərəns]   n. 保险

ore	[ɔː(r)]	n.	矿石
delicate	['delɪkət]	adj.	易碎的
voyage	['vɔɪɪdʒ]	n.	航行；航程
marine	[mə'riːn]	adj.	海运的
quotation	[kwəʊ'teɪʃn]	n.	报价单
consignment	[kən'saɪnmənt]	n.	托付物
urgent	['ɜːdʒənt]	adj.	紧急的

Notes

1. What insurance rate do you suggest we should acquire?
   您认为我们的保险费率应为多少？
2. Then am I right in understanding that FPA does not cover partial loss for the nature of particular average?
   投平安险则不包括单独海损的部分损失，我这样理解对吗？
3. A WPA policy covers you against partial loss in all cases.
   不管发生什么情况，投水渍险，将负责被保货物的部分损失。
4. Are you going to make an offer today?
   今天你们能报盘吗？
5. I'll immediately get the rate for you.
   我马上给你报保险费率。
6. CIF: Cost Insurance and Freight(成本、保险费加运费)，习惯上又称为"到岸价格"。
7. All Risks 一切险
8. FPA: Free from Particular Average 平安险
9. WA / WPA: With Average or With Particular Average 水渍险
10. SRCC: Strike, Riot and Civil Commotion 罢工、暴乱、民变险
11. TPND: Theft, Pilferage & Non-delivery 偷窃提货不着险
12. War Risks：战争险

【拓展音频】

Dialogue 2

W=Miss Wang   B: Mr. Brown

W: In terms of CIF, we would offer the particular average insurance for you. Do you have any specific requirements?

B: Could you tell me if the particular average insurance includes the compensation of damaged goods?

W: The compensation of damaged goods is covered in the insurance of risk of breakage. If you claim, the appended insurance will be added.

B: Are the customers responsible for the insurance charges?

W: Yes. This is standard practice.

B: What about the insurance for All Risks?

W: The insurance for All Risks will cover the compensation of damaged goods, but the premium is somewhat higher.

B: It doesn't matter. What we want to have is peace of mind.

Vocabulary

requirement	[rɪˈkwaɪəmənt]	n.	要求
breakage	[ˈbreɪkɪdʒ]	n.	破损
claim	[kleɪm]	n.	声称；索赔
append	[əˈpend]	v.	附加
premium	[ˈpriːmiəm]	n.	额外费用；奖金
compensation	[ˌkɒmpenˈseɪʃn]	n.	补偿

Notes

1. in terms of 依据；按照；在……方面

   For example: In terms of CIF, we would offer the particular average insurance for you.

   例如：按照 CIF 价格，我方可以为您投保单独海损险。

2. particular average insurance 单独海损险

   For example: Could you tell me if the particular average insurance includes the compensation of damaged goods?

   例如：请问单独海损是否包括货物破损的赔偿？

3. The compensation of damaged goods is covered in the insurance of risk of breakage.

   货物破损的赔偿属于破损险的责任范围。

4. If you claim, the appended insurance will be added.

   如果贵方要求的话，可以加保这项附加险。

5. This is standard practice.

   这是惯例。

6. The insurance for All Risks will cover the compensation of damaged goods, but the premium is somewhat higher.

   投保一切险的话，就包括了货物破损的赔偿，不过保险费也比较高。

【拓展音频】

Useful Sentences 常用口语

1. May I ask you a few questions about insurance?
   可以问您几个有关保险的问题吗?

2. What's the difference between FPA and WPA?
   平安保险与水渍险的区别是什么?

3. We shall cover the shipment for 110% above the invoice value.
   我们将按发票金额的110%投保。

4. We shall cover the goods against WPA and TPND risks.
   我们将为货物投保水渍险和偷窃提货不着险。

5. What sort of insurance policy have you secured?
   你投保哪种险?

6. Personally, I think the damage was due to careless packing.
   我认为损失是由于包装不当造成的。

7. I think the responsibility should rest with the shipping company.
   我认为责任方在于货运公司。

8. We agree with all the terms and conditions of the insurance contract.
   保险合同中的所有条款与条件均符合我们的要求。

9. Shall we attend to the insurance?
   是由我们投保吗?

10. Please consider the terms of the insurance contract that suit us.
    请考虑保险单中适合我们的条件。

11. What insurance rate do you suggest we should get?
    您认为我们的保险费率应为多少?

12. Obviously, you won't want All Risks cover.
    很显然,你们不会投一切险。

13. FPA will be good enough.
    投平安险就可以了。

14. Are there any other clauses in marine policies?
    海运保险中还有其他条款吗?

15. Could you give me a quotation for my consignment now?
    现在您能对我们的寄信货物做一下估价吗?

16. Are you going to make an offer today?
    今天你们能报盘吗?

17. I'll get the rate to you now.
    我马上给你报保险费率。

18. Do you have any specific requirements?
    您还有什么具体的要求吗？
19. This is standard practice.
    这是惯例。

 Further Reading 拓展阅读

Why You Need Insurance for Trade Show Exhibits

※ **Possible Dangerous Scenarios at Trade Show Booths**

People usually aren't consciously aware of all the possible dangers that can arise at any moments, especially at exhibition and shows. However, there is always the slight possibility that something catastrophic could occur, and for this reason, we purchase insurance. Consider an event specific to home improvement tools. If an exhibitor is demonstrating a chain saw, he could risk cutting off his own fingers. Should this happen he'd probably drop the saw and cause possible injury to nearby attendees.

There are many business sectors that contain the products that can be dangerous. Take for instance a trade show booth that is promoting knives and guns while exhibitors are extremely knowledgeable about their products, and know how to handle them safely, there is always the possibility that a show attendee could drop a knife on their foot, or even use it to hurt someone else. And the list goes on.

※ **Types of Insurance and What They Cover**

You should definitely purchase insurance to cover all of the previously mentioned scenarios. It is important to have insurance that covers you as the exhibitor, the exhibition attendees, the trade show booths' props and displays, and the building hosting the show.

When deciding on an insurance policy, it's crucial to check that the policy covers everything you will need. Normally, companies will offer both single event policies and annual event policies. Usually, these policies protect you from general liability, liabilities related to property damage, and losses or destruction of trade show exhibits, displays, and props. Some policies also cover medical expenses of event participants, event cancellation, or weather insurance. It is critical to find out what each policy you are considering covers, if there are any lapses in coverage, and if temporary guests and employees are covered.

When participating in trade show exhibits, it is essential to purchase insurance to cover any damages. New products on display could fail and cause injury, and you will want your company to be covered in case of an emergency.

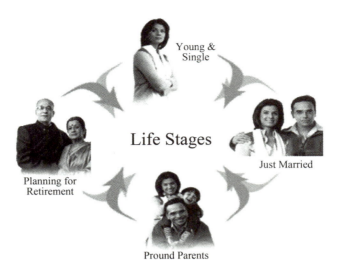

Vocabulary

consciously	[ˈkɒnʃəsli]	adv.	有意识地
catastrophic	[ˌkætəˈstrɒfɪk]	adj.	灾难的
saw	[sɔː]	n.	锯子
extremely	[ɪkˈstriːmli]	adv.	极其
scenario	[səˈnɑːriəʊ]	n.	情节；脚本
prop	[prɒp]	v.	支撑；维持
liability	[ˌlaɪəˈbɪləti]	n.	责任；债务
property	[ˈprɒpəti]	n.	财产
emergency	[iˈmɜːdʒənsi]	n.	紧急情况
expense	[ɪkˈspens]	n.	消费；开支
lapse	[læps]	n.	失效；流逝
temporary	[ˈtemprəri]	adj.	暂时的
essential	[ɪˈsenʃl]	adj.	必要的；本质的
destruction	[dɪˈstrʌkʃn]	n.	破坏

Notes

1. People usually aren't consciously aware of all the possible dangers that can arise at any moment, especially at exhibitions and shows.
   人们通常没有意识到随时可能发生的危险，尤其是在展会和展览中。

2. Normally, companies will offer both single event policies and annual event policies.
   通常，保险公司既提供单一活动保单，也提供年度活动保单。

3. Usually, these policies protect you from general liability, liabilities related to property

damage, and losses or destruction of trade show exhibits, displays, and props.

通常来说，这些保单保护你免于一般责任，财产损失相关责任以及损失或破坏贸易展会展品、展示用具的责任。

Answer the following questions.

1. What are the reasons to buy insurance for your trade show? Firstly make a list, and then give a brief explanation.

2. Summarizing the types of insurance with simple words.

Decide whether the following statements are True or False based on the above passage.

1. People can usually be aware of the dangers that can arise at any moment, especially at exhibits and shows. ( )

2. We purchase insurance because there is always the slight possibility that something catastrophic could occur at shows. ( )

3. There are a few business sectors that contain products that can be dangerous. ( )

4. When deciding on an insurance policy, there's no need to check that the policy covers everything you require. ( )

5. When participating in exhibitions, it is essential to purchase insurance to cover any damages. ( )

6. New products on display could fail and cause injury, and you will want your company to be covered in case of an emergency. ( )

Exercises

1. Match the words on the left with their proper meaning on the right.

(1) disaster　　　　a. an act of traveling by water

(2) moral　　　　　b. the act of decreasing or reducing something

(3) hazard　　　　 c. hand tool having a toothed blade for cutting

(4) saw　　　　　 d. a source of danger

(5) reduction　　　e. relating to principles of right and wrong

(6) voyage　　　　f. a state of extreme ruin and misfortune

(7) marine　　　　g. decide by reasoning

(8) urgent　　　　 h. the act of breaking something

(9) breakage　　　i. compelling immediate action

(10) conclude　　　j. of or relating to the sea

2. Read the following statements, and fill in the blank spaces with the appropriate words contained in the word box.

| due | transportation | due | protect | cover | attention |

(1) If we want an exhibition to be successfully staged, we should also focus our_____ on exhibitor's insurance.

(2) We need exhibitor's insurance to_____those unexpected misfortunes.

(3) Exhibitor's insurance is specially designed to _____exhibitors' displays or demonstrations.

(4) Exhibitor's insurance covers areas such as: lost expenses_____to cancellation of the exhibition.

(5) Delays in_____to the event.

(6) The core of the insurance is that it pays for loss exhibitors suffer as the result of disruption of the event_____to any cause beyond the control of exhibitors.

3. Translate the following sentences into English.
(1) 我认为展品损坏是由于包装不当造成的。
(2) 保险合同中的所有条款与条件均符合我们的要求。
(3) 很显然，你们应该投保一切险。
(4) 附加险的保险费由买方来负担。

4. Role play.

Work in pairs or more. Perform a short play according to the following instruction.

Suppose you find some of your exhibits missing. Discuss the problem with your insurance company, explaining how it happened, and whose responsibility it is, and solving the problem.

Practical Training Project 实训项目

Work in a group of 5. Your company is attending a trade show abroad in two months. Work out a plan describing the amount of insurance coverage you will need and then give a presentation on your plan to the whole class.

Unit 11

Contract Signing
签 订 合 同

Learning Objectives 学习目标

After learning this unit, you will be able to:
★ Understand the definition and legal effect of a contract.
★ Describe the necessary parts of a contract.
★ Be familiar with terms in a contract.
★ Grasp useful words and expressions concerning this topic.

Background Information 背景知识

合同是阐明有关各方必须履行的义务和责任的一种协议规定。会展合同对于调整会展各方之间的利益关系，明确各方的权利、义务，防止纠纷的产生，妥善处理会展中的问题，起着至关重要的作用。由于会展活动涉及会展组织者、参展商、场地提供者和观众等众多法律主体，他们之间的关系很复杂，因此根据合同主体的不同，广义的会展合同可以分为参展合同、场地提供合同、入场合同等。

Lead-in 导入活动

【拓展案例】

A contract is an agreement entered into voluntarily by two parties or more with the intention of creating a legal obligation.

An exhibition contract plays a vital role in linking the relationships among the relevant exhibition parties, clearly defining their respective rights, obligations, while avoiding disputes, and properly handling any issues that may occur at the Convention Hall and Exhibition.

A written contract generally involves the following parts: organizer of the exhibition, exhibitor, exhibition's detailed information, booth, booth location and exhibition fees, delivery and return of goods, insurance, cancellation policy, other agreements, duration of the contract and signatures, etc.

Unit 11

签订合同
Contract Signing

Warm-up 热身活动

Match and Discuss

Directions: Match the pictures in the left column with the corresponding terms in the right column. Discuss with your partner to determine how much you understand about each service.

1.    A. exhibition registration service

2.    B. exhibition logistics service

3.    C. booth construction service

4.    D. exhibition venue service

145

Basic Reading 基础阅读

Why Even a Simple Contract Can Prevent Problems?

Simply put, a contract is an enforceable agreement between two or more parties. The contract contains the promises made by the parties to one another, which is legally known as "consideration". These promises define the relationship being assumed as well as what happens if the business relationship doesn't work out. If one party fails to act according to their promises, then they have "breached" or broken the contract and can be found liable for damages. The damages typically equate to what the non-breaching party would have received if there had been no breach in the contract.

Oral Contract VS. Written Contract

You go to a social gathering with a friend and meet someone interested in your products or services. Eventually, you agree to provide him with 1 000 units of your products in exchange for a discounted price. You have created what is known as an "oral contract." He has promised to order products and you have promised to provide them at a discounted price. Is the agreement worth anything, or legally binding? Unfortunately, the answer is most likely "No". Why? In most situations, oral contracts are not enforceable if they have a value in excess of $500. Since it is very difficult to establish the actual terms of an oral contract that is in dispute, the legal system tries to discourage them. In fact, this legal restriction is generally known as the "Statute of Frauds".

With even a simple written contract, you can create a clause containing language that states you will give a 10 percent discount. If the dispute ends up in court, he is asked if his signature is on the contract. The clause is then read and you win. The contract should also contain a clause requiring the "prevailing party" to be reimbursed for their attorney's fees and costs. In short, he has to pay your legal bills as well.

An additional benefit to using a written contract is the due diligence section. I realize you will be shocked to learn that there are unethical businesses. In negotiating a contract, very specific requirements are put in writing. What if the other party starts squirming, or shows discomfort? It may be a sign they are unable to meet their obligations. This should concern you, and prevent you from continuing further negotiations with this company. You can save yourself numerous complications by realizing this potential problem in advance.

In summary, even a simple written contract should be a mandatory protection document. You will be glad you have one if a business transaction falls apart.

Unit 11

签订合同
Contract Signing

Vocabulary

enforceable	[ɪnˈfɔːsəbl]	adj.	可强迫的
breach	[briːtʃ]	v.	违反
liable	[ˈlaɪəbl]	adj.	可能（做某事）
discourage	[dɪsˈkʌrɪdʒ]	v.	阻碍
restriction	[rɪˈstrɪkʃn]	n.	限制
statute	[ˈstætʃuːt]	n.	法规
fraud	[frɔːd]	n.	欺诈
prevailing	[prɪˈveɪlɪŋ]	adj.	盛行的
reimburse	[ˌriːɪmˈbɜːs]	v.	补偿
attorney	[əˈtɜːni]	n.	律师
diligence	[ˈdɪlɪdʒəns]	n.	勤奋
unethical	[ʌnˈeθɪkl]	adj.	不道德的
squirm	[skwɜːm]	v.	扭动；不舒服
obligation	[ˌɒblɪˈgeɪʃn]	n.	义务
mandatory	[ˈmændətəri]	adj.	命令的

Notes

1. The contract contains the promises made by the parties to one another, which is legally known as "consideration".
   合同中包含了双方彼此做出的承诺，这个在法律上被称作"约因"。

2. These promises define the relationship being assumed as well as what happens if the business relationship doesn't work out.
   这些承诺确定了关系的建立以及如果贸易关系不能正常运行会发生什么。

3. If one party fails to act according to their promises, then they have "breached" or broken the contract and can be found liable for damages.

   如果一方不根据承诺履行合同，那么就"背弃"或违背了合同，应该承担损失赔偿责任。

4. The damages typically equate to what the non-breaching party would have received if there had been no breach in the contract.

   损失通常等同于如果合同没有被违背，非违约方将获得的利益。

5. In most situations, oral contracts are not enforceable if they have a value in excess of $500.

   在大多数情况下，如果口头合同价值超过 500 美元，就不能强制执行。

6. Since it is very difficult to establish the actual terms of an oral contract that is in dispute, the legal system tries to discourage them.

   因为存在争议的口头合同很难建立实际的条款，所以法律制度不提倡口头合同。

Discuss the following questions with your partner.

【拓展术语】

1. Please state the main difference between the written contract and the oral contract.
2. If you are a businessman, why do you think a contract is important?
3. What are the benefits of even signing a simple contract?

Situational Dialogues 情景对话

Dialogue 1

Mr. Brown, the manager of a Food & Beverage Company, is responsible for the food & beverage at an upcoming show. He is talking with the secretary of the show organizer, International Show Center, about amending a contract.

B= Mr. Brown   S=the secretary of the show organizer

B: Over the past couple of days I have closely read the contract draft.

S: Are there any questions?

B: Yes, there are a few points that I'd like to mention. The first one is about the packing. It's stipulated in the contract that all the machine parts should be packed in wooden cases. This can be done with the machine parts, but it's impossible to pack a truck base like that.

S: I see.

B: The second is about the terms of payment. The contract states that payment is to be

Unit 11

签订合同
Contract Signing

  made by D/P. This is not our practice. We prefer to have the payment made by L/C through a negotiation bank in France.

S: And…

B: And the third point is about arbitration. It's stipulated that arbitration shall take place in China. In all our previous contracts signed with you, it was stipulated that arbitration should take place in a third country.

S: Yes, that's right.

B: Why do you want it now mediated in China?

S: Shall we take up the matter point by point?

B: That's a good idea.

S: Now, the first point is about packing. We can approve a different packing for the truck bases.

B: Great!

S: Secondly, we agree to make the payment by L/C.

B: Thank you!

S: Due to our dealings with so many countries, we think it is best that all arbitrations are decided in China. The CCPIT arbitration commission enjoys a high prestige. I personally hope you'll accept this clause in the contract. Furthermore, any disputes that have arisen from our business transactions were all settled through friendly discussions. Very rarely has there been a need for arbitration.

B: I see. OK. The new arbitration clause is acceptable.

S: Is there anything else?

B: No, you have satisfied my concerns related to the contract terms. Thank you very much.

S: When should we sign the contract?

B: Can you have the final contract revisions ready by tomorrow morning? We can both sign the contract at that time.

S: Yes! See you tomorrow morning.

Vocabulary

secretary	['sekrətri]	n.	秘书
draft	[drɑːft]	n.	草稿
stipulate	['stɪpjuleɪt]	v.	规定
arbitration	[ˌɑːbɪ'treɪʃn]	n.	仲裁
commission	[kə'mɪʃn]	n.	委员会
prestige	[pre'stiːʒ]	n.	声望
furthermore	[ˌfɜːðə'mɔː(r)]	adv.	此外
dispute	[dɪ'spjuːt]	v.	对…提出质询；争论

transaction	[trænˈzækʃn]	n.	交易
consultation	[ˌkɒnslˈteɪʃn]	n.	咨询
revise	[rɪˈvaɪz]	v.	修正；校订

Notes

1. D/P : Documents against Payment 付款交单

2. L/C: Letter of Credit
   信用证，是国际贸易中最主要、最常用的支付方式。

3. In all our previous contracts signed with you, it was stipulated that arbitration should take place in a third country.
   在所有我们已签订的合同中都有规定，仲裁应在第三国进行。

4. Shall we take up the matter point by point?
   我们逐点研究一下，好吗？

5. The new arbitration clause is acceptable.
   这项新的仲裁条款是可以接受的。

6. CCPIT: China Council for the Promotion of International Trade
   中国国际贸易促进委员会

7. The arbitration commission of CCPIT enjoys a high prestige.
   贸促会仲裁委员会享有很高的威望。

8. Furthermore, the disputes that have arisen from our business transaction were all well settled through friendly consultations.
   此外，我们商业交易中出现的纠纷都通过友好协商的方式解决了。

【拓展音频】

Dialogue 2

Mr. Black, an exhibitor, is discussing about the proposed contract with Mr. White, the receptionist from the organizer of an Auto Show.

W=Mr. White   B=Mr. Black

W: We've prepared a rough draft of the contract. Please examine it at your earliest convenience.

B: May I ask a question about the proposed contract?

W: Yes. What is it?

B: Is there a specific time period you would like to have the contract validated?

W: Yes. How about one year to start?

B: We feel that a one-year contract is too short, and we propose at least a two-year contract.

Unit 11 签订合同 Contract Signing

W: That would be fine. And perhaps we could make it renewable for two-year periods contingent on the agreement of both parties.

B: I have one more question. Is it possible to terminate the contract after one year?

W: With a 6-month prior notice the contract can be cancelled. If both parties do not agree to renew the contract when the time comes, the agreement will automatically become void.

B: It's quite clear. I am satisfied with the terms of the contract for the most parts, but before signing it, I'd like to first review all the details. Is that OK?

W: Yes, but we would appreciate a quick response.

B: I'll do my best.

Vocabulary

examine	[ɪgˈzæmɪn]	v.	检查；审问
propose	[prəˈpəʊz]	v.	提议；建议
specific	[spəˈsɪfɪk]	adj.	特殊的；具体的
validate	[ˈvælɪdeɪt]	v.	证实；使生效
contingent	[kənˈtɪndʒənt]	adj.	偶然的
terminate	[ˈtɜːmɪneɪt]	v.	结束；终止
automatically	[ˌɔːtəˈmætɪkli]	adv.	自动地
void	[vɔɪd]	v.	无效的
response	[rɪˈspɒns]	n.	反应；回答

Notes

1. We've prepared a rough draft of the contract.
   我们已经准备了一份合同草稿。

2. Please examine it at your earliest convenience.
   请在您方便时尽早检查。

3. Is it possible to terminate the contract after one year?
   一年后可以终止合同吗？

4. I'll do my best.
   我会尽我所能。

【拓展音频】

Useful Sentences 常用口语

1. I have studied the draft contract you sent me. It's a good starting point, but no more than that.
   我已经仔细研究了您给我的合同草案，这是个良好的开端，但仅此而已。

2. I think it will have to be redrafted.
   我认为应该重新起草。

3. Could you explain what the last sentence on part 4 of the draft means? It does not seem to make sense.
   您能解释一下合同草案的第4部分最后一句话是什么意思吗？似乎没什么意义。

4. I have brought a draft contract, please have a look. Please let us know if you have any questions.
   我已经带来了合同草案，请过目。如果有任何不清楚的地方请告诉我们。

5. When should we sign the contract?
   我们什么时候可以签合同？

6. We will revise the contract today, and have it ready to be signed tomorrow. Will that be OK?
   我们今天将对合同进行修改，明天就可以签，怎么样？

7. Do you have a sample contract?
   贵方有合同样本吗？

8. It seems that we can't reach an agreement on this point.
   在这一点上我们似乎无法达成共识。

9. If everything is satisfactory, we can draw up a formal contract.
   如果一切都满意，我们就能起草一份正式合同了。

10. The contract can be cancelled by mutual agreement.
    在双方都同意的前提下可以取消合同的履行。

11. In case one party fails to carry out the terms of the contract, the other party is entitled to cancel the contract.
    如果一方不执行合同，另一方有权撤销该合同。

12. This contract will be in force as soon as it is signed by both parties.
    合同经双方签订即可生效。

Further Reading 拓展阅读

What Makes a Quality Business Agreement – or a Contract?

The contract is the foundation of doing business. Does that sound too formal to you? Is a handshake agreement good enough for many? Even though it may not be as secure as a contractor

Unit 11
签订合同
Contract Signing

agreement, a handshake deal is still a contract. The moment two people agree to a price for exchange of goods and services, they have entered into a legal contract. That is why knowledge of contracts, and the issues involved, should be important to all people in business. Knowing the differences between a good and bad contract can protect your interests.

In fact, knowing more about contracts is like knowing more about life and history in general. Contract law is certainly not the creation of a few thoughtful individuals, nor a part of any kind of grand design. Indeed, contract law has much of its roots in the common law foundation of American society.

That is, contract law is somewhat a textbook example of how common law developed in Britain and the United States. People engage in business transactions. Eventually, some of these become sources of disputes between various parties. Some laws, already on the books, may cover the dispute. Very often, they don't. So that's where a court needs to get involved to cover so-called tricky cases and establish new laws.

It is the desire to avoid grey areas, and matters of interpretation, which creates the need to form contracts to protect your interests. In other words, a handshake can get you in trouble, since the specifics of such a contract can be a matter open to interpretation. What is less open to interpretation is a legal contract or contractor agreement that specifically states the obligations of all parties of a contract. The more the contract clearly outlines these obligations, the better off all parties will be, especially if there is a dispute.

It's not just the simple exchange of goods and services for a fee that are subject to contractual arrangements. There are numerous components of business and relevant activities that come under the umbrella of contracts.

If you want to outsource your activities to someone else, that's a contract. If you hire people for a period of time, that's a contract. If you hire people to fix something in your office, that's a contract. Almost any decisions to form an arrangement with someone else, especially when money is involved, can form the basis of a contractual arrangement carrying with all the duties and obligations of a legal contract.

Another way of putting it is this: If you're doing business with anyone to any degree, there's a contract involved somewhere. And if it could potentially impact you and your business, you better get it down on paper. Some contracts may not need to be as formal as a contractor agreement, but the more specific a legal contract is, then the better position you can be in to protect your interests, and that of your business.

Perhaps nowhere is this truer than with respect to the contractor agreement. Companies are hired to do all types of projects for all kinds of clients. If someone wants to contract for your services, and pay you a lot to do it, then you should already have a prepared contractor agreement that covers both of your interests. It lets the client know that they are dealing with a good contractor, while also protecting you from somebody who plays loose with the notion of what a business contract is.

Vocabulary

foundation	[faʊnˈdeɪʃn]	n.	基础
formal	[ˈfɔːml]	adj.	正式的
handshake	[ˈhændʃeɪk]	n.	握手
engage	[ɪnˈɡeɪdʒ]	v.	从事
tricky	[ˈtrɪki]	adj.	棘手的
interpretation	[ɪnˌtɜːprəˈteɪʃn]	n.	阐明
contractor	[kənˈtræktə(r)]	n.	立契约者
component	[kəmˈpəʊnənt]	n.	构成要素
outsource	[ˈaʊtsɔːs]	v.	外购
notion	[ˈnəʊʃn]	n.	观念

Notes

1. That is why knowledge of contracts, and the issues involved, should be important to all people in business.
那就是合同知识和相关问题对于所有商业人士都重要的原因。

2. Contract law is certainly not the creation of a few thoughtful individuals, nor is it part of any kind of grand design.
合同法既不是几个深思熟虑的人的创造，也不是任何宏伟设计的一部分。

3. Indeed, contract law has much of its roots in the common law foundation of American society.
合同法实际上是在美国社会普通法的基础上建立起来的。

4. That is, contract law is somewhat a textbook example of how common law developed in Britain and the United States.
也就是说，合同法从某种程度上来说像是一个文本示例，展示了普通法在英国和美国是如何发展起来的。

Unit 11 签订合同 Contract Signing

5. So that's where a court needs to get involved to cover so-called tricky cases and establish new laws.

   所以，这就是法院需要参与，去解决所谓的棘手案件并且建立新法律的地方。

6. It is the desire to avoid grey areas, and matters of interpretation, which creates the need to form contracts to protect your interests.

   为了避免灰色区域和问题解释，因此产生了建立合同保护自身利益的需要。

Answer the following questions.

1. Why are contracts important in business?
2. What do you think of the handshake agreement?

Decide whether the following statements are True or False based on the above passage.

1. When two people reach an oral agreement, it becomes a legal contract. (   )
2. Knowing more about life and history means knowing more about contracts. (   )
3. In American society, contract law is as important as common law. (   )
4. The more the contract clearly outlines these obligations, the less trouble all parties will have in the event of a dispute. (   )
5. A contract is really useful when somebody plays tricks with you. (   )
6. Most of contracts don't need to be as formal as a contractor agreement. (   )

Exercises

1. Match the words on the left with their proper meaning on the right.

   (1) contain   a. the act of rewriting something
   (2) party   b. being ahead of time or need
   (3) handshake   c. financial assistance in time of need
   (4) engage   d. a proportion multiplied by 100
   (5) oral   e. set up or found
   (6) establish   f. using speech rather than writing
   (7) percent   g. carry out or participate in an activity
   (8) benefit   h. grasping and shaking a person's hand
   (9) advance   i. a group of people who are involved in an activity together
   (10) revise   j. include or contain

155

2. Read the following statements, and fill in the blank spaces with the appropriate words contained in the word box.

| contract | agreement | parties | attached | writing | oral |

(1) A contract is a legally binding document or agreement between multiple _____.

(2) An oral contract is an _____ that outlines the terms of a contract through spoken communication.

(3) In essence, an oral contract is an affirmed _____. However, the only difference is the way in which the agreement is delivered.

(4) In an oral contract, written or physical evidence of the stipulations can be _____ to the oral agreement.

(5) The oral contract is not written, but the evidence attached to the agreement can be affirmed through _____.

(6) An _____ contract, although not as formal or traditional as a written contract, has been used for multiple landmark agreements.

3. Translate the following sentences into English.

(1) 合同中如果有任何不清楚的地方请马上告诉我们。

(2) 合同经双方签字就具有法律效力。

(3) 在谈判双方都同意的前提下可以取消合同的履行。

(4) 在这一点上我们似乎无法达成共识。

4. Role play.

(1) Suppose you are the organizer of a trade show. It is a Saturday morning and you have an appointment with an exhibitor who wants to know something about the contract. You give him the detailed information. Make a dialogue.

(2) Suppose you are the sales manager of a company. Your company wants to sign a contract with the client early tomorrow morning. The client and you are now negotiating specific details of the contract on the telephone. Make a dialogue.

Practical Training Project 实训项目

Do some research on the Internet and learn about the following types of international contracts.

Sole Agency Contract

Sole Distribution Contract

Unit 11
签订合同
Contract Signing

Contract for Assembling
Contract for Compensation Trade
Private Consulting Contracts

Choose one type of contract you are really interested in. Find a sample contract, and make a presentation explaining the clauses in detail.

Unit 12

Handling Complaints
处 理 投 诉

Unit 12

处 理 投 诉
Handling Complaints

Learning Objectives 学习目标

After learning this unit, you will be able to:
★ Understand the reasons for customer complaints.
★ Make oral complaints.
★ Know how to handle customer complaints.
★ Master useful words and expressions concerning this topic.

Background Information 背景知识

会展是一个系统的服务提供过程，涉及多方参与者：主办方、参展商、行业协会、主场搭建商、会展运输商、会展中心（会展场所提供方）、目标观众等。在这样一个庞大的工程中，总是不可避免地存在一些服务上的问题，使得观众和参展商产生抱怨。如有的参展商抱怨参展费用太高、设备耽搁、服务差，甚至有时观众还会与参展商发生冲突等。这时，当事各方往往会向主办方求助。在会展活动中，不论考虑得多么周到，组织得多么完美，顾客投诉都是必然的。因此，如何妥善处理投诉，考验着主办方的智慧。

Lead-in 导入活动

【拓展视频】

After the event, customers may sometimes complain to the organizer about the high cost of attending a show, the delay of the equipment though the staffs of organizer have tried their best to explain the reasons, and solve the problems if possible. Sometimes, some event visitors may have some disputes with the exhibitors. They may also turn to the organizer for their assistance to solve the problems. In business activities, no matter how hard-working an organization may be, it is certain that complaints may arise from the customers. The buyers at times may find that the goods they have purchased not be as good as they thought. So in most cases, buyers will choose to write a complaint to the suppliers.

Warm-up 热身活动

Match and Discuss

Directions: Please look at the following pictures and read the descriptions of the procedure for dealing with complaints. Match each picture with the correct description.

1.    A. Call the customer a few days later to see if they are satisfied with their replacement products.

2.    B. Apologize for their inconvenience and concerns.

3.    C. Greet the customer with a smile and tell them your name.

4.    D. Summarize the problem back to them to ensure you have all the facts, and reassure that you have been listening to them.

5.    E. Give them something extra (an upgraded product, a discount on their next service, or a voucher they can use on their next purchase).

Unit 12
处 理 投 诉
Handling Complaints

6.  F. Record details about the complaint, such as customer's name and contact details, the product or service, how you dealt with it and how the customer reacted.

 Basic Reading 基础阅读

How to Deal with Customer Complaints?

Complaints are a part of the business, and knowing how to deal with them will only serve to make your business stronger. If you want to learn the secrets of handling customer complaints better, follow these tips.

Recognize Complaints as Opportunities for Growth

Sure, it's difficult to accept being shouted at as a positive thing, but it is sometimes necessary. Of course, customers won't always raise their voices, but the way they deliver their complaints isn't always the point. It is what they are saying that needs to register in your mind.

If you're too sensitive, you'll probably never be able to survive operating a business. Instead of taking the objections personally, think of complaints as a means to improve your products or your service.

Record the Nature of the Complaint

Don't let any complaints go without an appropriate response. Handling customer complaints must include writing down the major points as a record for future reference.

Doing this also shows your customers that you acknowledge what they have said, and that you will definitely do something about it.

Follow up on the Issue

By now, you should have already resolved or have done something to correct the problem. However, that is not where your service ends.

Handling customer complaints doesn't stop when you have responded to an issue. You still must continue to communicate with the complainants to determine if he or she is satisfied with the corrective action.

Many businesses do not bother to do this, but be assured that these gestures are very much appreciated. Following up makes the customers feel that they're really being taken care of, and that you value their business.

You may not think that you (or your employees) need to learn the details of handling customer complaints. What you may not realize is that the way you deal with these matters will also have a very positive impact on your company.

Professionally handling customer complaints will reflect very well on the kind of person you are, and the kind of company you work for. In contrast, dealing with customer objections as if they don't really matter will also reveal a negative aspect of how you do business.

Vocabulary

recognize	['rekəgnaɪz]	v.	承认
sensitive	['sensətɪv]	adj.	敏感的
survive	[sə'vaɪv]	v.	活下来
objection	[əb'dʒekʃn]	n.	异议
reference	['refrəns]	n.	参考
acknowledge	[ək'nɒlɪdʒ]	v.	承认
contrast	['kɒntrɑːst]	n.	对比
bother	['bɒðə(r)]	v.	打搅
gesture	['dʒestʃə(r)]	n.	姿势
impact	['ɪmpækt]	v.	影响
reveal	[rɪ'viːl]	v.	显示
professionally	[prə'feʃənəli]	adv.	专业的

Notes

1. Complaints are a part of the business, and knowing how to deal with them will only serve

to make your business stronger.
投诉是商业活动的一部分，知道如何处理投诉将会有助于企业的强大。

2. It is what they are saying that needs to register in your mind.
   你需要把他们说的事情记在心中。

3. Many businesses do not bother to do this, but be assured that these gestures are very much appreciated.
   许多企业不想这样麻烦，但是这样的行为会得到极大的赞赏。

4. In contrast, dealing with customer objections as if they don't really matter will also reveal a negative aspect of how you do business.
   相反，在处理客户异议的时候表现得好像他们根本不重要，这暴露出你进行商业活动的消极一面。

Discuss the following question with your partner.

Why is dealing with a complaint so important?

【拓展术语】

Situational Dialogues 情景对话

Dialogue 1

The following conversation is between a company staff member and a customer, concerning a complaint or claim.

S=staff   C=customer

C: I want to have your opinion related to a quality issue concerning our recent receipt of your goods.

S: Sorry, but we guarantee there is nothing wrong with our products.

C: Well, there is a serious damage with three boxes of glassware, and I think it's customary for us to ask for compensation.

S: It is impossible for our company to accept the responsibility the during transportation. Furthermore, the quality of goods is the responsibility of the C&F company. Therefore, we are not responsible for any shipping quality issues.

C: Does that mean we should ask for compensation from the insurance agent?

S: I believe that is correct.

Vocabulary

| claim | [kleɪm] | n. 声称；索赔 |

guarantee	[ˌɡærənˈtiː]	n.	保证
glassware	[ˈɡlɑːsweə(r)]	n.	玻璃器皿
compensation	[ˌkɒmpenˈseɪʃn]	n.	赔偿金
insurance	[ɪnˈʃʊərəns]	n.	保险
responsible	[rɪˈspɒnsəbl]	adj.	负责的
transportation	[ˌtrænspɔːˈteɪʃn]	n.	运输

Notes

1. I want to have your opinion related to a quality issue with regards our recent receipt of your goods.
   对于我们收到的货物质量问题，我想听听你的意见。
2. It is impossible for our company to accept the responsibility during the transportation.
   对运输途中发生的损失进行赔偿是我们公司不能接受的。
3. furthermore 此外
4. be responsible for 对……负责
5. insurance agent 保险公司

【拓展音频】

Dialogue 2

C: We received your digital cameras yesterday. The shipping boxes were damaged, in which the digital cameras were packed.

S: I'm sorry to hear that. How much is the do you estimate total damage?

C: Over 150 cameras are missing or stolen.

S: I apologize for the damage, and the problems this has caused you.

C: We'll send you a list of the damaged and missing items.

S: OK. Do you want us to send you another shipment as per your last order? We presently have lots of digital cameras in stock.

C: Please wait for our list of items that we want to replace. You can then ship them to us at your earliest convenience.

S: We will wait for your list of items, and immediately send you the replacements.

C: Thank you so much!

Vocabulary

digital	[ˈdɪdʒɪtl]	adj.	数字的
camera	[ˈkæmərə]	n.	照相机

Unit 12
处理投诉
Handling Complaints

pack	[pæk]	v.	包装
estimate	['estɪmət]	v.	判断；评价
stock	[stɒk]	n.	股份；库存
article	['ɑːtɪkl]	n.	文章；物品
shipment	['ʃɪpmənt]	n.	装货
apologize	[ə'pɒlədʒaɪz]	v.	道歉

Notes

1. digital camera 数码相机
2. How much do you estimate is the total damage?
   您估计全部损失有多少？
3. I apologize for the damage, and the problems this has caused you.
   我对造成的损害和存在的问题向您道歉。
4. We'll send you a list of the damaged and missing items.
   我们会寄给你一份损坏和丢失货品的清单。
5. Do you want us to send you another shipment as per your last order?
   您要我们按您的订单重新发一批货吗？
6. in stock 有现货的；有库存的
   For example: We have lots of digital cameras in stock now.
   我们现在有很多数码相机的存货。

【拓展音频】

Useful Sentences 常用口语

1. We assume that damage occurred while the consignment was in your care.
   我们认为货物是在你方保管时受到损坏的。
2. We reserve the right to claim compensation.
   我方保留索赔的权利。
3. We will entertain your claim after the retained samples are rechecked.
   在保留样品经过再检验之后，我们将答复你方的索赔要求。
4. You will have a reply in 3 days.
   3 天后你们就能收到答复。
5. After making a thorough investigation, we have decided to accept your claim and to compensate you for the amount of lost goods.
   经过详细调查后，我方决定受理你方索赔并赔偿有关的损失。

6. We will compensate for your loss, if we find that we were at fault.
   如果责任在我方，我们会对你方的损失进行赔偿的。

7. We have never had a complaint of this kind.
   我们从未收到过这样的投诉。

8. We do not provide the compensation for any loss in transit.
   我们不接受运输中任何损失的赔偿。

9. You should ask the insurance company for the compensation.
   你们应该向保险公司索赔。

10. Sorry, but we cannot accept your claim.
    很抱歉，我们不能受理你们的索赔。

11. We disclaim any responsibilities for it.
    我们不承担任何责任。

12. It seems that we have to withdraw the claim.
    看来我们不得不撤回索赔要求了。

 Further Reading 拓展阅读

How to Write a Complaint Letter?

Writing a complaint letter is often an unpleasant task, but if it is done well, the end result can be very rewarding. Often a complaint letter is more effective than a simple phone call or for e-mail message. When writing your complaint letter, it's best to identify a defined purpose and outcome that you want to achieve, and indicate those ideas clearly in your letter.

Then, how do you write a complaint letter? How many parts does it consist of?

Normally, a complaint letter will include your name, address, and home & work phone numbers.

Type your letter if possible. If it is handwritten, make sure it is neat and easy to read.

Make your letter brief and to the point. Include all important facts about your purchase, including the date and place where you made the purchase and any information you can give about the product or service, such as serial, model numbers or specific type of service.

State exactly what you want done about the problem and how long you are willing to wait to get it resolved.

Be reasonable. Include all documents regarding your problem. Be sure to send COPIES, not originals.

Avoid writing an angry, sarcastic, or threatening letter. The person reading your letter probably was not responsible for your problem but may be very helpful in resolving it.

Keep a copy of the letter for your records.

Unit 12
处 理 投 诉
Handling Complaints

※ **Sample Complaint Letter**

  Name of Contact Person, if available

  Title, if available

  Company Name

  Consumer Complaint Division, if you have no contact person

  Street Address

  City, State, Zip Code

  Dear (Contact Person)

  Re: (account number, if applicable)

  On (date), I (bought, leased, rented, or had repaired) a (name of the product, with serial or model number or service performed) at (location and other important details of the transaction).

  Unfortunately, your product (or service) has not performed well (or the service was inadequate) because (state the problem). I am disappointed because (explain the problem: for example, the product does not work properly, the service was not performed correctly, I was billed the wrong amount, something was not disclosed clearly or was misrepresented, etc.).

  To resolve the problem, I would appreciate it if you could (state the specific action you want—money back, charge card credit, repair, exchange, etc.). Enclosed there with are copies of my records (include copies of receipts, guarantees, warranties, canceled checks, contracts, model and serial numbers, and any other documents).

  I look forward to your reply and a resolution to my problem, and will wait until (set a time limit) before seeking help from a consumer protection agency or the Better Business Bureau. Please contact me at the above address or by phone at (home and/or office numbers with area code).

  Sincerely,

  Your name

  Enclosure(s) cc: (reference to whom you are sending a copy of this letter, if anyone)

Vocabulary

handwritten	[ˌhænd'rɪtn]	adj.	手写的
neat	[niːt]	adj.	灵巧的；整洁的
serial	['sɪərɪəl]	adj.	连续的；分期偿还的
specific	[spə'sɪfɪk]	adj.	特殊的；详细的
original	[ə'rɪdʒənl]	n.	正本；原稿
sarcastic	[sɑː'kæstɪk]	adj.	讽刺的
threatening	['θretnɪŋ]	adj.	胁迫的
division	[dɪ'vɪʒn]	n.	分类
inadequate	[ɪn'ædɪkwət]	adj.	不够格的
disclose	[dɪs'kləʊz]	v.	使显露公开
misrepresented	[ˌmɪsˌreprɪ'zentɪd]	adj.	不如实叙述的
enclosed	[ɪn'kləʊzd]	v.	附上
receipt	[rɪ'siːt]	n.	收据；收条
warranty	['wɒrənti]	n.	保单担保
resolution	[ˌrezə'luːʃn]	n.	解决方案

Notes

1. When writing your complaint letter, it's best to identify a defined purpose and outcome that you want to achieve, and indicate those ideas clearly in your letter.
   当写投诉信的时候，你最好确定一个你想实现的目标和结果，并且在信里把这些想法都说清楚。

2. State exactly what you want done about the problem and how long you are willing to wait to get it resolved.
   准确地陈述你希望如何解决问题以及你可以等待多长时间让问题得到解决。

3. Include all documents regarding your problem.
   包括关于你的问题的所有文件资料。

4. Avoid writing an angry, sarcastic, or threatening letter.
   避免写一封带有愤怒、讽刺或威胁的信。

5. The person reading your letter probably was not responsible for your problem but may be very helpful in resolving it.
   阅读你信件的人很可能不负责你的问题，但是有可能帮助你解决问题。

Answer the following questions.

1. How many parts does a complaint letter consist of?

Unit 12
处理投诉
Handling Complaints

2. What are the tips on writing a complaint letter? Please give a brief explanation on them.

Decide whether the following statements are True or False based on the above passage.

1. Writing a complaint letter is often an unpleasant task. ( )
2. Often a simple phone call is more effective than a complaint letter. ( )
3. When writing your complaint letter, it's best to identify a defined purpose and outcome that you want to achieve in your letter. ( )
4. Make your letter sharp and to the point. ( )
5. The person reading your letter probably was not responsible for your problem but may be very helpful in settling it. ( )
6. State exactly what you want done about the problem and ask them to solve the problem as soon as possible. ( )

Exercises

1. Match the words on the left with their proper meaning on the right.

(1) handle   a. take the trouble to do something
(2) apologize   b. of greater importance
(3) improve   c. have as a part
(4) include   d. to make better
(5) major   e. acknowledge faults or shortcomings or failing
(6) bother   f. be in charge of
(7) realize   g. make visible
(8) reflect   h. the opposition
(9) contrast   i. manifest or bring back
(10) reveal   j. be fully aware

2. Read the following statements, and fill in the blank spaces with the appropriate words contained in the word box.

| kind | gift | business | complaints | possible | happy |

(1) It is important to handle customer _____ properly.

(2) You want to keep customers _____ otherwise they will most likely stop shopping there at your company.

(3) Make sure to take their complaints seriously. Show that you care about the issue and want

to improve the situation as quickly as _____.

(4) You want them to know that you care. Be friendly, smile, and be _____.

(5) You need to make sure to give them a free _____ card or major discount in order to make up the complaints.

(6) You want them to feel happy enough to want to do _____ with your company again.

3. Translate the following sentences into English.

(1) 我们从来没有收到过这样的投诉。

(2) 我对你们的产品质量和服务质量都不满意。

(3) 我们会做一个全面彻底的调查，找出真正的责任所在。

(4) 我期待着您的答复，并妥善解决我的问题。

4. Role play.

Work in pairs or more. Try to do a short play according to the following instructions.

Suppose you are complaining to the organizer of the show about the poor condition of the video equipment they provided. Try to get their explanations and solutions.

Practical Training Project 实训项目

1. Mrs. Helen tries to explain every aspect of the events leading up to her claim. She brings everything to Mr. Wang, including a survey report, an inspection report, and the contract. But, Mr. Wang states his company's decision to firmly reject the claim. Mrs. Helen is very angry. Imagine yourselves to be Mrs. Helen and Mr. Wang. Design your own conversation between them.

2. Mrs. Helen has no other alternative but to submit the matter to arbitration. At the court hearing, both Mrs. Helen and Mr. Wang present their positions and evidence concerning the case. After the arbitrator's analysis, a final decision and settlement is announced.

Divide yourselves into small groups and play the roles of Mrs. Helen, Mr. Wang and the arbitrators. Make your presentations of the court hearing, including the final decision and the settlement.

Unit 13

Exhibition Dismantling
撤 展

Learning Objectives 学习目标

After learning this unit, you will be able to:
★ Know the exhibit dismantling procedures.
★ Know what to do with the dismantling display items.
★ Know how to express your gratitude to the exhibition organizer.
★ Master the useful expressions for moving out of an exhibition.

Background Information 背景知识

一般而言，展会闭幕标志着本届展会正式结束。然而，展会闭幕并不意味着展会现场工作就此结束。展会闭幕后，展会的撤展工作还需要办展机构进行必要的管理。

展会的撤展工作主要包括展位的拆除、参展商租用展具的退还、参展商展品的处理和回运、展场的清洁和撤展安全保卫等工作。

Lead-in 导入活动

【拓展视频】

On the last day of the trade show, exhibitors need to express their appreciation to the people that have helped them during the show, including people that have assisted with the display items, dismantling, rentals, transportation, checking out, etc.

Warm-up 热身活动

Match and Discuss

Directions: Match the pictures in the left column with the activities in the right column,

Unit 13
Exhibition Dismantling 撤展

and discuss with your partner to determine how much you understand about exhibit dismantling activities.

1.    A. express gratitude to the organizer

2.    B. showing customer appreciation

3.    C. exhibit transportation

4.    D. exhibit dismantling

 Basic Reading 基础阅读

How to Reduce Damage to Your Trade Show Exhibit Items During Post-show Dismantling?

Most trade shows are open for 3 or 4 days. If you have ever been on the show floor, during the last few hours, you will see an amazing transition taking place.

A week earlier there was an air of excitement and urgency as the exhibit crates were delivered to the booth spaces. Prior to opening the show the installation crews will urgently work to get everything in place.

In contrast, by afternoon on the last day of the show, the booth staff is tired, the traffic is light and everyone is ready to rush to the airport. Often, the booth staff will be required to stay after the show closes to assist in dismantling the booth. It is fitting to say that they most likely will not use the same care in dismantling the booth as they did in setting it up. Expensive display components are often carelessly placed into the shipping containers.

In the end, what seems like a great way to save money will instead result in costing you dearly. In my experience, there are ways to reduce the chances of damage during post-show dismantling. The first would be to pay an installation and dismantling company to dismantle and pack the booth. This is not always feasible, especially if you personally set up the booth. If you cannot hire someone, then designate one or two members of your staff to stay at least one extra day to take care of dismantling the display. If your people know that they are not going to be departing the night the show closes, they will be much more likely to take their time when packing the display.

A good double check is to have the display thoroughly inspected upon its return. If it has been improperly packed, you will want to know about it immediately so that you can have it repaired before its next use.

Vocabulary

reduce	[rɪˈdjuːs]	v.	减少
damage	[ˈdæmɪdʒ]	v.	损毁
dismantle	[dɪsˈmæntl]	v.	拆除
urgency	[ˈɜːdʒənsi]	n.	紧急
crate	[kreɪt]	n.	板条箱
installation	[ˌɪnstəˈleɪʃn]	n.	安装
crew	[kruː]	n.	全体人员

Unit 13 撤展 Exhibition Dismantling

contrast	['kɒntrɑːst]	v.	对比
component	[kəm'pəʊnənt]	n.	成分
container	[kən'teɪnə(r)]	n.	集装箱
feasible	['fiːzəbl]	adj.	可行的
designate	['dezɪgneɪt]	v.	指派
extra	['ekstrə]	adj.	额外的
inspect	[ɪn'spekt]	v.	检查
immediately	[ɪ'miːdiətli]	adv.	立即

Notes

1. A week earlier there was an air of excitement and urgency as the exhibit crates were delivered to the booth spaces.
   在展会召开前一周，当展品箱被送到展位的时候，一种兴奋和紧张的气氛油然而生。

2. In contrast, by afternoon on the last day of the show, the booth staff is tired, the traffic is tight and everyone is ready to rush to the airport.
   相比之下，到了展会最后一天的下午，展位的工作人员都累了，交通也很拥挤，大家都准备赶往机场。

3. It is fitting to say that they most likely will not use the same care in dismantling the booth as they did in setting it up.
   他们在拆除展位的时候，很可能不会像他们搭建展位时那样小心谨慎。

4. In the end, what seems like a great way to save money will instead result in costing you dearly.
   最终，看似省钱的方法反而会让你付出高昂的代价。

5. The first would be to pay an installation and dismantling company to dismantle and pack the booth.
   首先是付钱给安装和拆卸公司，请他们拆除并包好展位。

Discuss the following question with your partner.

What seems like a great way to save money and reduce the damage to your trade show exhibit?

【拓展术语】

 Situational Dialogues 情景对话

Dialogue 1

Miss Li comes to Mr. Zhang's booth on the last day of trade show. She expresses her appreciation of Mr. Zhang's products. At the same time, she offers her own suggestions.

  L =Miss Li   Z=Mr. Zhang

L: Good morning, Mr. Zhang.

Z: Good morning, Miss Li. I'm so happy to see you again. I remember you came to our booth on the first day of the show.

L: Yes, I'm here again because your silk products are very appealing to me.

Z: Do you like the products we sold you?

L: Yes. The silk cheongsam are selling well, especially the ones with the traditional Chinese patterns and characters.

Z: I'm glad to hear that. I'll send you a catalogue of our various products when I go back to my country.

L: Thank you very much. In this show, your products, presentation, and hospitality really impressed me. By the way, if your silk products have brighter colors, they will be more popular.

Z: I'm glad you have a good impression of our products, Miss Li. I will also tell my general manager about your suggestion. I hope we can keep in touch and continue to work together. Our phone numbers and E-mail address are on the booklet I gave you.

L: I will stay in touch with you. Have a safe and happy journey home!

Vocabulary

appeal	[əˈpiːl]	n.	请求；吸引力
cheongsam	[tʃɒŋˈsæm]	n.	旗袍
character	[ˈkærəktə(r)]	n.	特性
catalogue	[ˈkætəlɒg]	n.	目录
presentation	[ˌpreznˈteɪʃn]	n.	陈述
hospitality	[ˌhɒspɪˈtæləti]	n.	好客
booklet	[ˈbʊklət]	n.	小册子

Notes

1. appealing to: 对……有吸引力的

   For example: I'm here again because your silk products are very appealing to me.
   例如：我又来了，因为你们的丝绸制品对我很有吸引力。

【拓展音频】

2. In this show, your products, presentation, and hospitality really impressed me.
   在这次展览会中，你们的产品、展示，还有你的热情款待都给我留下了很深的印象。

3. I'm glad you have a good impression of our products.
   很高兴我们的产品给您留下这么好的印象。

Unit 13

撤 展
Exhibition Dismantling

4. general manager (GM)：总经理

5. I hope we can keep in touch and continue to work together.
希望我们能继续保持联系，并进一步合作。

Dialogue 2

After the trade show, Miss Liu is expressing her appreciation to Ada, who is a member of the organizing committee of the trade show and who has been a great help to Miss Liu. At the same time, Miss Liu is busy preparing to return to her country.

L=Miss Liu   A=Ada

L: Good afternoon, Ada. Thank you very much for your great help during the trade show.

A: It's my pleasure. I appreciated your way of doing business. If there is anything else I can do for you, please don't hesitate to let me know.

L: In fact, I really need your help.

A: What is it?

L: What should I do with the display items?

A: You can sell some of the display items. For those that you cannot sell here, you can find a transportation company to ship them back to your country.

L: That sounds good. Which transportation company do you recommend?

A: We have already appointed a few transportation companies. Here are their telephone numbers.

L: Thank you. I will call them right away.

Vocabulary

appreciate	[ə'priːʃieɪt]	v.	欣赏
hesitate	['hezɪteɪt]	v.	犹豫
recommend	[ˌrekə'mend]	v.	推荐
appoint	[ə'pɔɪnt]	v.	指定；任命

Notes

1. I appreciated your way of doing business.
我非常欣赏你高效的工作方式。

2. If there is anything else I can do for you, please don't hesitate to let me know.
如果还有什么事需要我帮忙，请不要客气。

3. Which transportation company do you recommend?
您能帮我推荐一家运输公司吗？

【拓展音频】

4. We have already appointed a few transportation companies.
这次展览会组织者指定了几家运输公司。

Useful Sentences 常用口语

1. In this show, your products, presentation, and hospitality really impressed me.
   在这次展览会中，你们的产品、展示，还有你的热情款待都给我留下了很深的印象。
2. I'm glad you have a good impression of our products.
   很高兴我们的产品给您留下这么好的印象。
3. I hope we can keep in touch and continue to cooperate.
   希望我们能继续保持联系，并进一步合作。
4. Our phone numbers and E-mail address are on the booklet I gave you.
   我给您的小册子上有我们的电话号码和电子邮件地址。
5. Thank you for your help during the exhibition.
   谢谢您在展会期间的帮助。
6. I appreciated your way of doing business.
   我非常欣赏您高效的工作方式。
7. If there is anything else I can do to help you, please don't hesitate to let me know.
   如果还有什么事需要我帮忙，请不要客气。
8. In fact, there is something I am still not sure about.
   实际上，我还有一件事不太明白。
9. What should I do with the display items?
   我该如何处理这些展品呢？
10. You can sell some of the display items. For those that you cannot sell here, you can find a transportation company to ship them back to China.
    你可以将一部分展品在这里出售，另外再找一家运输公司，将不能出售的部分运回中国。
11. Which transportation company do you recommend?
    您能帮我推荐一家运输公司吗？
12. We have already appointed a few transportation companies. Here are their telephone numbers.
    这次展览会组织者指定了几家运输公司。这是他们的联系方式。

Further Reading 拓展阅读

Necessary Departure Procedure

For any big event, like the recently concluded 7th China International Cultural Industries Fair,

Unit 13
撤 展
Exhibition Dismantling

there should always be a systematic method to end the event. May 16 is the last day for the ICIF. This is also the time to prepare the booths for departure. The exhibitors should also be prepared to leave the event.

Departure time will begin after the closing ceremonies on May 16, and will continue until the next day, May 17. Exhibitors with the Release Pass for Goods out of Exhibition Hall are permitted to leave with their exhibit products and equipment. The departure procedure involves the responsibility of the people involved with each exhibition. They should comply with the provisions set by the Organizing Committee Office in moving the exhibits out of the halls. Another part of the agreement is that the exhibitors shall not be allowed to depart from the halls until the duration of the fair. The release pass will only be issued after the end of the fair.

The departure time will begin at 5:30 in the afternoon, after the closing ceremonies, and will continue until the next day from 8:30 in the morning until 5:30 in the afternoon. An Approval List for Exhibits Moving out of the Exhibition Hall must be presented in order to get all the necessary articles out of the halls. This document must have the authorized signature of the site official. Exhibitors need to assign personnel for each booth to look after the articles in the exhibit to ensure that no items will be missing during and after the exhibition period. Their role is very important, especially in the moving in and the moving out process, since the list of items will be checked during each period.

Proper management of the exhibition involves the security of the booths and the exhibits, management of the articles, and security while promoting and expanding knowledge to the fair participants. For any loss or damage that may occur during the exhibition period, the ICIF Company will not be held liable. This is usually included in the contractual agreement.

The exhibitors, participants, and personnel should be responsible to keep the exhibition in an orderly manner, and avoid unnecessary incidents and illegal activities that can compromise the entire exhibition event.

The participants and personnel for each booth and exhibit should wear their respective badges at all times. This will allow easier tracking and managing of the booths for the officials and security personnel. The badges should not be given to others, and should not be abused by using it other than its intended purpose. For those who do not comply, the officials will take the necessary action for any violation incurred. For delivery trucks and other vehicles, the necessary permits should be ready upon moving in and out. Permits for moving into the exhibit are different from the permits for moving out. It is also important that the specified exit routes be followed to ensure smooth traffic flow for all vehicles.

Vocabulary

systematic	[ˌsɪstəˈmætɪk]	adj.	系统的
permit	[pəˈmɪt]	v.	许可；允许
equipment	[ɪˈkwɪpmənt]	n.	设备
provision	[prəˈvɪʒn]	n.	供应品
duration	[djuˈreɪʃn]	n.	持续
approval	[əˈpruːvl]	n.	批准
document	[ˈdɒkjumənt]	n.	文件
authorized	[ˈɔːθəraɪzd]	adj.	经授权的
signature	[ˈsɪgnətʃə(r)]	n.	署名
security	[sɪˈkjʊərəti]	n.	安全
expand	[ɪkˈspænd]	v.	扩张；使膨胀
occur	[əˈkɜː(r)]	v.	发生；出现
liable	[ˈlaɪəbl]	adj.	有义务的
respective	[rɪˈspektɪv]	adj.	各自的
badge	[bædʒ]	n.	徽章；证章
abuse	[əˈbjuːs]	v.	滥用；辱骂
violation	[ˌvaɪəˈleɪʃ(ə)n]	n.	违反
vehicle	[ˈviːəkl]	n.	交通工具

Notes

1. Exhibitors with the Release Pass for Goods out of Exhibition Hall are permitted to leave with their exhibit products and equipment.
   有《商品移出展厅许可证》的参展商，可以将参展产品和设备带出场馆。

Unit 13
撤 展
Exhibition Dismantling

2. They should comply with the provisions set by the Organizing Committee Office in moving the exhibits out of the halls.

   他们应该遵守组委会办公室制定的规定，把展品带出展厅。

3. The release pass will only be issued after the end of the fair.

   通行证只在展会结束之后发放。

4. An Approval List for Exhibits Moving out of the Exhibition Hall must be presented in order to get all the necessary articles out of the halls.

   要想把必要的物品带出展厅，必须出示展品移出展厅批准清单。

5. For delivery trucks and other vehicles, the necessary permits should be ready upon moving in and out.

   运输卡车和其他车辆应该获得必要的许可才能进出展厅。

6. For those who do not comply, the officials will take the necessary action for any violation incurred.

   对于不遵守规定的人员，官方将会对发生的任何侵害行为采取必要行动。

Answer the following questions.

1. What are the exhibit dismantling procedures? Make a list.
2. What should we do when dismantling the display items?

Decide whether the following statements are True or False based on the above passage.

1. Sometimes, the participants and personnel for each booth and exhibit should wear their respective badges. (　　)

2. The badges could be given to others. (　　)

3. Permits for moving into the exhibit are similar to the permits for moving out of the exhibit. (　　)

4. The release pass will be issued during the fair. (　　)

5. The exhibitors shall not be allowed to depart from the halls until the duration of the fair. (　　)

6. The departure procedure involves the responsibility of the people involved with each exhibition. (　　)

Exercises

1. Match the words on the left with their proper meaning on the right.

(1) exhibit   a. the act of hiring something or someone

(2) dismantle   b. in place of

(3) urgent   c. an abstract part of something

(4) prior   d. give help or assistance

(5) installation   e. the act of moving hurriedly

(6) rush   f. the act of installing something

(7) assist   g. earlier in time

(8) component   h. the state of being urgent

(9) instead   i. take off or remove

(10) hire   j. something shown to the public

2. Read the following statements, and fill in the blank spaces with the appropriate words contained in the word box.

faster	detailed	advance	money	error	intact

(1) When you work with an Install and Dismantle company at your next trade show, it is important to have full communications with them so that your trade show exhibit will remain _____.

(2) If these trade show exhibit items are included in detail, there is less chance for _____.

(3) By giving this information to your trade show exhibit installer, they will be able to do their job more efficiently, saving your time and _____.

(4) Since everyone is in a hurry as the trade show move-in date gets closer, having a list on hand in _____ will help ensure a worry-free trade show booth installation on the trade show floor.

(5) Remember that a descriptive and _____ inventory list can save your time and money and ensure that your trade show booth remains intact.

(6) The more information your I & D handler has, the _____ they will be able to do their job. If you take the mystery out of your trade show exhibit assembly, you will win the day.

3. Translate the following sentences into English.

(1) 通常来说，工作人员在拆卸展位时不如搭建展位时用心。

(2) 在这次展会中，你们的产品以及你们的热情款待都给我留下了很深的印象。

(3) 这次展会组织者指定了几家运输公司。

(4) 我非常欣赏你有条不紊的工作方式。

4. Role play.

Work in pairs or more. Try to do a short play according to the following instruction.

Suppose you are watching labor people dismantle your exhibition display. When you see that they are not being very careful with the equipment, then how can you correct their actions without causing an embarrassing situation?

Practical Training Project 实训项目

Do some Internet research, involving specific information concerning departure from an exhibition. Prepare an 8-minute presentation showing the procedure for exhibit dismantling on behalf of the event exhibitor.

Unit 14

Contacting after the Exhibition
展 后 联 系

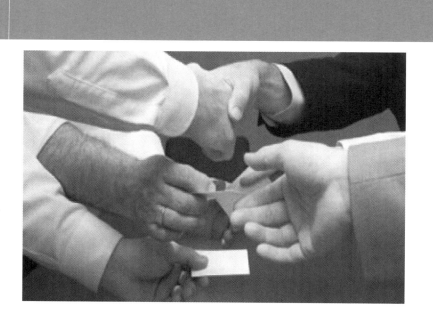

Unit 14

展 后 联 系
Contacting after the Exhibition

Learning Objectives 学习目标

After learning this unit, you will be able to:
★ Learn exhibition follow-up strategy.
★ Follow up sales orders placed at the exhibition.
★ Follow up with potential clients.
★ Learning useful words and expressions concerning this topic.

Background Information 背景知识

展会结束后，要分析评估展会的效果、参展企业是否达到了预期目标以及订单的跟进与处理等。因此，需要进行一系列的展后联系活动。

(1)对客户及潜在客户寄送感谢卡、寄送产品资料和样本、及时回复客户的问题、邀请客户进行座谈、销售业务代表继续跟进客户和潜在客户。

(2)给新闻界寄发感谢卡或感谢信。此外，还要对参展经验进行总结，对参展活动进行评估，以便为下次参展提供借鉴和依据。

Lead-in 导入活动

【拓展视频】

The end of a trade show doesn't mean the end of an exhibitor's work. After the show, it is also important to get in touch with visitors and potential customers to make them real buyers, and also the time to consider further enhancing your product quality, or services.

Generally speaking, the follow-up business of an exhibition should include:
◇ Send samples or catalogues to customers or potential customers.
◇ Have a conference with potential clients.
◇ Representatives pursue further marketing activities.
◇ Summarize the show.

Warm-up 热身活动

Match and Discuss

Directions: Match the pictures in the left column with their activities in the right column and discuss with your partner to see how much you understand about follow-up activities.

1.    A. send thank you cards

2.    B. press release

3.    C. discussing exhibition follow-up strategies

4.    D. making follow-up telephone calls after the show

Unit 14
展后联系
Contacting after the Exhibition

Basic Reading 基础阅读

The Importance of Exhibition Follow-Up

In an increasingly hostile global financial and business market, businesses have to look for new ways to generate business or maximize the existing marketing methods. While it is true that many businesses do already use exhibitions as a means of generating new business but many fail to maximize the potential of such events. Although, exhibition follow-up is both tiresome and somewhat boring at times it is a necessary for any business however large or small. It is the contacts and prospective customers from these functions that will make your business flourish and progress it to the next level.

A clear and targeted follow-up strategy is required if you are to turn the interest into sales and results. You can simply have the exhibition and expect the business to start rolling in. But, you do need to actively pursue any leads that you may have, and soon eliminate those that have little interest. There is no point wasting the valuable and expensive time of your sales people on leads that are simply not interested in what you have to offer. With a well-designed follow-up telephone campaign, you could be making large gains with a relatively small investment, while potentially taking customers away from your competition.

Finally, while you may think that the point of an exhibition is to generate new business, it is also designed to maintain the confidence and loyalty of your existing customers. Be sure not to neglect your loyal customers! If done properly and efficiently, follow-up can make exhibitions a very cost-effective marketing tool.

Vocabulary

hostile	[ˈhɒstaɪl]	adj.	不友好的
financial	[faɪˈnænʃl]	adj.	金融的
generate	[ˈdʒenəreɪt]	vt.	使形成；发生；生殖
maximize	[ˈmæksɪmaɪz]	v.	达到最大值
tiresome	[ˈtaɪəsəm]	adj.	令人厌倦的
flourish	[ˈflʌrɪʃ]	v.	繁荣；兴旺
eliminate	[ɪˈlɪmɪneɪt]	v.	消除
neglect	[nɪˈglekt]	v.	忽视；忽略
maintain	[meɪnˈteɪn]	v.	维持
confidence	[ˈkɒnfɪdəns]	n.	信心
loyalty	[ˈlɔɪəlti]	n.	忠诚
campaign	[kæmˈpeɪn]	n.	活动；战役

Notes

1. Although, exhibition follow-up is both tiresome and somewhat boring at times it is a necessary for any business however large or small.
   虽然，有时候展会的后续工作既累人又无聊，但是，这项工作对业务是十分必要的。

2. A clear and targeted follow-up strategy is required if you are to turn the interest into sales and results.
   如果你想要把那些兴趣点转化为销售业绩和成果，就需要一个明确的和有目标的跟进策略。

3. You can simply have the exhibition and expect the business to start rolling in.
   你可以只是举办展览会，就期望生意开始兴隆起来。

4. There is no point wasting the valuable and expensive time of your sales people on leads that are simply not interested in what you have to offer.
   销售人员把宝贵时间浪费在那些对你的产品根本不感兴趣的客户身上，是没有意义的。

5. If done properly and efficiently, follow-up can make exhibitions a very cost-effective marketing tool.
   如果后续工作做得正确有效，会使展会成为划算的营销手段。

Discuss the following questions with your partner.

【拓展术语】

1. Why is follow-up so important?
2. What should you do after a trade show?

Unit 14

展后联系
Contacting after the Exhibition

 Situational Dialogues 情景对话

Dialogue 1

Kenny Watson, the manager of an exhibitor, is talking with one of the venue staff, Oliver Yang, about their products and booking a booth in advance for next year's show.

W=Kenny Watson   Y=Oliver Yang

Y: Good morning. This is the Beijing International Expo Center. This is Oliver Yang speaking. How may I assist you?

W: Good morning, Mr. Yang. This is Kenny Watson. I'm calling to thank you for your excellent assistance during the recent trade show.

Y: It's my pleasure to have been of some assistance.

W: From the feedback, we know that many clients were extremely impressed by our products, our presentation and hospitality.

Y: Yes, you have an excellent service with few that can match all you do.

W: In my opinion, the show went well, but we were not there to just make an immediate sale. We are also interested in finding new contacts, and create long term sales. The good news for you is that I'm going to attend the exhibition next year.

Y: Wonderful!

W: Can I now book a booth on the ground floor for next year?

Y: Yes, of course.

W: Great! I'd like to reserve booth number A6 on the ground floor.

Y: No problem. Booth A6 on the ground floor is available at this time.

W: I will confirm the booking by fax within one week. I am sure our company will get a lot of exposure again next year. Thank you very much.

Y: I'm glad I can help. Thank you for your participation.

Vocabulary

assistance	[əˈsɪstəns]	n.	帮助
feedback	[ˈfiːdbæk]	n.	反馈
hospitality	[ˌhɒspɪˈtæləti]	n.	好客
confirm	[kənˈfɜːm]	v.	确认
exposure	[ɪkˈspəʊʒə(r)]	n.	曝光
reserve	[rɪˈzɜːv]	v.	预订

Notes

1. It's my pleasure to have been of some assistance.
   我很高兴能对你有所帮助。
2. From the feedback, we know that many clients were extremely impressed by our products, our presentation and hospitality.
   据反馈得知，我们的产品介绍和热情接待给客户留下了深刻的印象。
3. in advance 事先；预先；提前
   For example: Can I now book a booth on the ground floor for next year?
   我现在就可以预订明年一层的展位吗？
4. Booth A6 on the ground floor is available at this time.
   位于一层的展位 A6 这时候还没有被预订。

【拓展音频】

Dialogue 2

J=John Campbell (Supplier)　　　P=Paul Smith (Buyer)

J: Hello Paul, this is John Campbell.

P: Hello, John, my friend.

J: How was your trip home?

P: Very good. Thank you for asking.

J: Are you satisfied with our products?

P: Up to now, we believe that your product quality is good, with a reasonable price and is very user-friendly.

J: Excellent news! This information is very important to us. We are encouraged to work harder to guarantee a good quality to all of our clients.

P: It has been decided that we will maintain a long-term business relationship with your firm.

J: This is very encouraging, and we will continue in our efforts to always improve.

P: We plan to place an order for ten thousand units with your company next year. Hopefully we will continue to have a good relationship with your company.

J: I really appreciate that. As a good customer we will consider giving you a volume discount with this big order. Wish you have a prosperous future and a long lived friendship with us.

P: We thank your company for offering us a very positive contract.

J: We are pleased to receive your comments or suggestions at any time. Meanwhile, we will follow our contract concerning the quality of our products, and listen to all meaningful suggestions from the clients. You are welcome to visit our facilities at any time.

P: I will. Thank you for your call. See you.

J: Thank you for being a satisfied customer. Take care.

Vocabulary

encourage	[ɪnˈkʌrɪdʒ]	v.	鼓励
extra	[ˈekstrə]	adj.	额外的
advantage	[ədˈvɑːntɪdʒ]	n.	优势；利益
comment	[ˈkɒment]	n.	评论
positive	[ˈpɒzətɪv]	adj.	积极的
prosperous	[ˈprɒspərəs]	adj.	繁荣的
satisfied	[ˈsætɪsfaɪd]	adj.	感到满意的

Notes

1. Are you satisfied with our products?
   你对我们的产品满意吗？

2. up to now 到目前为止

   For example: Up to now, we believe that your product quality is good, with a reasonable price and is very user-friendly.
   例如：到目前为止，客户反映产品的质量好，价格合理且实用。

3. long-term business relationship 长期的业务关系

   For example: It has been decided that we will maintain a long-term business relationship with your firm.
   例如：我们公司决定和贵公司保持长期的业务关系。

4. We will consider giving you a volume discount with this big order.
   我们可以考虑给贵方更多的优惠。

5. Wish you have a prosperous future and a long lived friendship with us.
   祝您前程似锦，我们的友谊长存。

【拓展音频】

 Useful Sentences 常用口语

1. I'm calling to thank you for your excellent assistance during our trade show.
   我打电话来是想对您在商展期间给我们的帮助说声谢谢。

2. It's a pleasure to have been of some assistance.
   我很高兴能对您有所帮助。

3. From the feedback, we know that many clients were deeply impressed by our products, our presentation and hospitality.

据反馈得知，我们的产品介绍和热情接待给客户留下了深刻的印象。

4. How are the responses to our products from the clients?
   使用我们的产品后客户反映怎么样？
5. Up to now, we have been told that the quality is good with reasonable price and practicality.
   到目前为止，客户反映产品的质量好，价格合理且实用。
6. It has been decided that we will maintain the long-term business relationship with your firm.
   我们公司决定和贵公司保持长期的业务关系。
7. We may even consider in giving you some extra advantage of this big order.
   我们可以考虑给贵方更多的优惠。
8. We hope you will continue to give us your active support, and we're looking forward to seeing you at the next show.
   希望您继续积极支持我们，并期待下次展会再见。
9. We hope you have a prosperous future and a long lived friendship with us.
   我谨代表我们公司祝贵公司事业蒸蒸日上，我们的友谊长存。
10. I really appreciate your cooperation, and hope you can join us at our next show.
    非常感谢您的合作，希望您参加我们举办的下次展会。
11. This is a card has the names of our sales staff.
    这是我们公司的贺卡，上面有我们全体销售部门人员的签名。
12. Thank you for your valuable time.
    谢谢您的宝贵时间。

Further Reading 拓展阅读

Pre-show Planning Leads to Post-show Success

While you're planning for the show, it's also a good time to plan for what happens after the show. Planning ahead of time for what your organization will do, after the event ends, is one of the most important pre-show activities. And executing that post-show follow-up in a timely fashion can mean the difference between new and lost sales.

Typically, companies participate in trade shows, or host seminars, in order to generate new leads. But more often than not, these same companies do not plan – before the show - how they will act upon those leads once the events have ended.

We've all heard the stories about companies who spent many thousands of dollars to participate in, or put on an event, only to lose millions in deals because they were so engrossed with staging the event, they "forgot" to plan the follow-up with prospects they met at the show.

To ensure your organization achieves a return on its investment, it is important to implement a pre-show plan that will detail what your organization will do after the event is over.

A company meeting with key personnel should occur before the event to set a goal for the

Unit 14
展后联系
Contacting after the Exhibition

show (i.e., number of meetings or leads desired), as well as determine how to handle post-show follow-up. What constitutes a lead? What do you do with the information from the lead sheets or automated card reader? Who gets the data? How will the prospects be cultivated? Will they be called? Which sales rep calls them? Will they be sent direct mail literature? This literature, or information, should actually be developed with your pre-show promotional package so it's ready to go before you even get to the show.

Companies often walk out of events with boxes of leads under their arms that never see the light of day. Typically, these pieces of paper land in a closet or in someone's bottom desk drawer. The person who brought the leads back is usually not responsible for lead follow up and is typically too busy with other activities to give attention to yesterday's events. These leads can sit there for months or much longer. Finally, somebody finds it. Then no one knows what to do and opportunities are already lost to competition. Pre-show planning avoids these types of problems.

The idea of the plan is to ensure that the few "pots of gold" are pursued and hopefully turned into clients. We've all heard horror stories in which companies have developed hundreds of leads, only to put them aside and forget about them. Eventually, somebody finds the box of leads. When the company finally initiates the post-show follow-up, they find that many of the prospects have since bought from a competitor. The company could have generated significant revenue had they planned ahead of time.

Companies need to remember the goal of any event is to generate new business. Preparation pays when it comes to getting the biggest return on investment at any technology event. Once it's over, you've already planned your post-show follow-up so implementation is easy when you return to the office.

Other after show activities include reviewing the event with key personnel to evaluate how well the show went, what mistakes were made, and determine how to fix any negatives for next time. Additionally, every technology firm should track budgets back to their original estimates, maintain a record of those budgets and settle their accounts. Over time, you'll be better able to track expenses and forecast costs for future shows. You will also be able to determine which shows are generating solid leads and revenue by monitoring and tracking leads back to each event.

Vocabulary

execute	['eksɪkjuːt]	v.	实施
seminar	['semɪnɑː(r)]	n.	专题讨论会
engross	[ɪn'ɡrəʊs]	v.	全神贯注
implement	['ɪmplɪment]	v.	贯彻
personnel	[ˌpɜːsə'nel]	n.	人员
constitute	['kɒnstɪtjuːt]	v.	构成
cultivate	['kʌltɪveɪt]	v.	培育
rep	[rep]	n.	推销人；代表
horror	['hɒrə(r)]	n.	恐怖
initiate	[ɪ'nɪʃieɪt]	v.	开始
estimate	['estɪmət]	v.	评价；判断
forecast	['fɔːkɑːst]	v.	预测

Notes

1. Planning ahead of time for what your organization will do, after the event ends, is one of the most important pre-show activities.
   提前规划好展会结束后贵公司的工作，是展会前的重要活动之一。

2. And executing that post-show follow-up in a timely fashion can mean the difference between new and lost sales.
   并且在展会后及时地展开后续工作，意味着是形成新交易还是失去交易。

3. But more often than not, these same companies do not plan – before the show - how they will act upon those leads once the events have ended.
   但是，这些同类型的公司经常不会计划——在展会前——一旦展会结束了，他们将如何处理那些商机。

4. What do you do with the information from the lead sheets or automated card reader?
   你将如何处理来自于宣传单和自动读卡器的信息？

5. The idea of the plan is to ensure that the few "pots of gold" are pursued and hopefully turned into clients.
   这个计划是要确保对这些"宝藏"进行后续跟踪，并且使其成为实际客户。

Answer the following questions.

1. If you are an exhibitor, what should you do before a trade show, and after a trade show?
2. What is the importance of a Pre-show planning?

Unit 14

展后联系
Contacting after the Exhibition

Decide whether the following statements are True or False based on the above passage.

1. Before holding an exhibition, the planner doesn't need to plan post-show activities. (   )
2. Before holding a show, the organization should hold a meeting with key personnel to set a goal for the show. (   )
3. Other after-show activities should include reviewing the event with key personnel to evaluate how well the show went, what mistakes were made, and determine how to fix it for next time. (   )
4. Leads brought back after a show should be kept in a closet. (   )
5. The pre-show plan can ensure that the few "pots of gold" are pursued and hopefully turned into clients. (   )
6. Companies need to remember the goal of any event is to generate new business. (   )

Exercises

1. Match the words on the left with their proper meaning on the right.

(1) global   a. get something
(2) generate   b. make more firm
(3) evaluate   c. the quality of being loyal
(4) method   d. lack of attention and due care
(5) customer   e. group of people willing to obey orders
(6) personnel   f. someone who pays for goods or services
(7) neglect   g. a way of doing something
(8) loyalty   h. place a value on
(9) confirm   i. bring into existence
(10) receive   j. involving the entire earth

2. Read the following statements, and fill in the blank spaces with the appropriate words contained in the word box.

| leads | up | clients | show | visitors | strategy |

(1) An awful lot of work goes into marketing your business at an exhibition or trade _____.

(2) You spend time and energy planning your marketing _____, designing and ordering your banner stands and graphics.

195

(3) At the event itself, you and your team work incredibly hard to attract _____ to your display stands and promote your products or services.

(4) You give away promotional items and marketing materials, as well as making valuable contacts and impressing prospective _____.

(5) To ensure that your hard work pays off, however, it is very important that you follow _____ on your trade show appearance when the event is over.

(6) Your exhibition appearance is likely to have generated _____ and prospects, but immediately after the show is the most opportune time to turn these into sales.

3. Translate the following sentences into English.

(1) 我们的产品介绍和热情接待给客户留下了极为深刻的印象。

(2) 客户反映我们的产品不仅质量好，而且价格合理。

(3) 我们公司决定和贵公司保持长期的业务关系。

(4) 我们经过讨论，一致同意给予贵方更多的优惠。

4. Role play.

(1) Suppose you are an organizer of a show, explain to your team what you should do to maintain a good business relationship with exhibitors after the show.

(2) Mr. James, marketing department manager at an exhibition and conference management company, is expressing his thanks to all the exhibitors at the conclusion of the show.

Practical Training Project 实训项目

Work in a group of 6. You all work in the Marketing Department. Your company attended a trade show last week. Discuss and decide a trade show follow-up plan and carry out the plan by phone calls, E-mails or letters. The students in other groups are your prospects or customers. Present your plan to the audience.

Unit 15

Exhibition Assessment
展会评估

Learning Objectives 学习目标

After learning this unit, you'll be able to:
★ Know the importance and necessities of exhibition assessment.
★ Know the basic definition and methodologies for exhibition evaluation.
★ Analyze the results of your exhibition experience.
★ Know how to organize and present the results of an exhibition.

Background Information 背景知识

会展评估是对会展活动的展览环境、工作效果等方面进行系统、客观、真实、深入的考核和评价，并做出权威的反馈。它是会展整体运作管理中的一个重要环节，是对主办单位、参展商和会展主管部门三方负责的执行性活动。当前，会展评估在世界会展经济发达国家已经相当成熟，在这些国家通常是全国性统一的行业机构从事展会的评估认证工作，对各类数据进行审核认证，定期公布认证结果，为会展业内和其他相关机构提供比较分析。

Lead-in 导入活动

【拓展知识】

The exhibition assessment should include:
◇ Selecting the standard of evaluation.
◇ Collecting information: collecting past information, writing on-site surveys, making questionnaires, holding meetings.
◇ Transferring information to statistics and analyzing them.
◇ Producing an analysis report.

Unit 15

展会评估
Exhibition Assessment

Warm-up 热身活动

Match and Discuss

Directions: Match the pictures in the left column with their activities in the right column and discuss with your partner to see how much you understand about the essentials of exhibition assessment.

1.    A. make a follow-up phone call

2.    B. write a business report

3.    C. press release

4.    D. questionnaire survey

How to Measure the Success of an Exhibition

The way you measure the success of an exhibition, in simple terms, is how much business can be related back to monetary value that will actually come from the event. Fairs, shows and exhibitions offer the best opportunity you could possibly imagine, only if you make them pay. Where else could you meet and talk to 50, 100, 200 or more new contacts in such a short period of time? Exhibitions present you with a huge business opportunity, but it really is up to you to maximize its potential.

※ **Track Your Budget**

Keep track of your budget and after the show is over, calculate a figure that includes absolutely everything you spent.

※ **Count Contacts or Leads**

Count the contacts or leads that were gained at the show and you can establish your cost per contact by dividing the total cost of the show by the total number of leads.

※ **Count Orders**

Keep track of the revenue gained as a result of the show and you can calculate your return on investment or ROI.

※ **Calculate Your ROI**

You will need to put a price, or value on your success. If it is recruiting new people, then how much would that cost using a different method? Possibly $4 000 if you used an agency. If you were to recruit 10 people, then you have a value of $40 000. Then divide your total value by the total budget i.e., divide $40k revenue by $10k cost and you get 4. Or simply put, the company has achieved four times return on investment.

※ **Create a Base for Measurement**

Knowing how well you have done gives you a benchmark to work from and improve upon.

Unit 15

展会评估
Exhibition Assessment

Vocabulary

measure	['meʒə(r)]	v.	测量；估量
maximize	['mæksɪmaɪz]	v.	最大化
potential	[pə'tenʃl]	adj.	潜在的
track	[træk]	n.	行踪；轨道
budget	['bʌdʒɪt]	n.	预算
calculate	['kælkjuleɪt]	v.	计算
figure	['fɪgə(r)]	v.	计算；出现
revenue	['revənjuː]	n.	收入；税收
recruit	[rɪ'kruːt]	v.	征募；吸收
benchmark	['bentʃmɑːk]	n.	基准

Notes

1. The way you measure the success of an exhibition, in simple terms, is how much business can be related back to monetary value that will actually come from the event.
   简单来说，衡量一个展会是否成功的标准，是有多少商业活动能与该展览实际产生的货币价值相关联。

2. Fairs, shows and exhibitions offer the best opportunity you could possibly imagine, only if you make them pay.
   交易会、展览和展会为你提供能想像到的最好的机会，只要你能使他们付钱。

3. Exhibitions present you with a huge business opportunity, but it really is up to you to maximize its potential.

展览会给你带来巨大的商机，但是确实是由你来最大限度地发挥它的潜力。

4. Count the contacts or leads that were gained at the show and you can establish your cost per contact by dividing the total cost by the total number of leads.
计算出你在展会上获得的交易数量，你就能通过用总成本除以总交易量得出每笔交易的成本。

5. Or simply put, the company has achieved four times return on investment.
或者简单地说，该公司已经实现了 4 倍的投资回报。

6. Knowing how well you have done gives you a benchmark to work from and improve upon.
知道你的表现如何，会给你提供一个基准来改进。

Discuss the following question with your partner.

【拓展术语】

How do companies usually measure the exhibition results? Is it effective?

Situational Dialogues 情景对话

Dialogue 1

Mr. Wang just participated in an international trade show. He is discussing the results of the trade show with the general manager, Mr. Feng.

W=Mr. Wang,　　F=Mr. Feng

F: Mr. Wang, what are the results of the trade show?

W: Not bad.

F: Could you give me some details?

W: We have established business relationships with ten new clients, who have now ordered 60 million RMB of cotton shirts.

F: Good.

W: I also got acquainted with more than 300 customers.

F: Oh, wow.

W: Our customers have made numerous suggestions. At the show, I held a product demonstration meeting, and a press conference. As a result, our brand name has been strengthened.

F: Great!

W: Here are the results of my analysis. I believe that the visitors at the show can become our new customers in 3 to 6 months. Furthermore, we learned a lot from viewing other exhibitors.

F: You are right. I think you've done an excellent job.

Unit 15

展会评估
Exhibition Assessment

Vocabulary

establish	[ɪˈstæblɪʃ]	v.	建立
acquaint	[əˈkweɪn]	v.	使熟悉
client	[ˈklaɪənt]	n.	客户
numerous	[ˈnjuːmərəs]	adj.	很多的
demonstration	[ˌdemənˈstreɪʃn]	n.	示范
strengthen	[ˈstreŋθn]	v.	增强

Notes

1. establish business relationships with… 与……建立业务关系

   We have established business relationships with ten new clients.
   我们与十个新客户建立了业务关系。

2. get acquainted with… 相识；熟悉；了解……

   I also got acquainted with more than 300 customers.
   我们还认识了 300 多名顾客。

3. strengthen (v.): to become stronger, or make something stronger 加强, 变坚固

   As a result, our brand name has been strengthened.
   因此，我们的品牌得到了加强。

4. At the show, I held a product demonstration meeting, and a press conference.
   在展会上我召开了产品展示会和新闻发布会。

【拓展音频】

Dialogue 2

After a trade show, Mr. Li, the general manager of the Splendor Fashion Company, is talking with Mr. Wang, a senior marketing expert, about their business situation.

L=Mr. Li   W=Mr. Wang

L: Good morning, Mr. Wang. I have some good news to tell you.

W: Oh. Please be seated. I learned that you have been doing quite well recently.

L: Yes, that's what I want to discuss with you. Our orders have doubled after the show, and we are currently still receiving orders. Most of the new buyers are visitors we met during the show. Our displayed items gave them an excellent impression. Now we can say that the show has been a success.

W: That's really exciting. By the way, what are you going to do at the next show?

L: We are making preparations for that now. We plan to make a brochure of our products and run some advertisements during the show. This will allow potential customers to know more about our company. We will still hold a press conference, which I think is very effective to promote our products. Do you think it's necessary to prepare some gifts for the next show?

W: That's a good idea. It's worthwhile to do that. You really learned a lot from the show. Good luck to you.

Vocabulary

original	[ə'rɪdʒənl]	adj.	最初的
situation	[ˌsɪtʃu'eɪʃn]	n.	局面
currently	['kʌrəntli]	adv.	目前
impression	[ɪm'preʃn]	n.	印象
brochure	['brəʊʃə(r)]	n.	小册子
worthwhile	[ˌwɜːθ'waɪl]	adj.	值得做的

Notes

1. Our orders have doubled after the show.
   展会后我们的订单翻了一倍。
   在此句中，double 作动词用，意为"使(某物)加倍；把(某物)增一倍"。
   For example: Our orders have doubled after the show.
   展会后我们的订单增加了一倍。

2. press conference 新闻发布会
   For example: We will still hold a press conference.
   我们还会举行新闻发布会。

3. promote product 促销产品
   For example: Which I think is very effective to promote our products.
   我认为这对推销我们的产品非常有效。

【拓展音频】

 Useful Sentences 常用口语

1. What are the results of the exhibition?
   这次展览效果如何？
2. Could you give me some details?
   您能否讲得更具体些？

3. We have established business relationships with many new clients.
   我们和许多新客户建立了贸易关系。

4. I also got acquainted with lots of new customers.
   我还结识了大批新客户。

5. Customers have made numerous suggestions.
   客户们提了许多建议。

6. Our brand has been strengthened.
   品牌得到了进一步的强化。

7. Here is the results analysis.
   这是效果分析。

8. I hope the visitors at the exhibition can be our real buyers in 3 to 6 months.
   我期望3~6个月后展会的参观者会成为我们真正的买家。

9. I think you've done an excellent job.
   我认为你们的工作完成得很好。

10. In this exhibition, your products, presentation, and hospitality really impressed me.
    在这次展览会中，你们的产品、展示，还有你的热情款待都给我留下了很深的印象。

11. I'm glad you have a good impression of our products.
    很高兴我们的产品给您留下这么好的印象。

12. I hope we can keep in touch and continue to cooperate.
    希望我们能继续保持联系，并进一步合作。

 Further Reading 拓展阅读

The Investigation Report on 2010 Changchun International Auto Expo

Introduction

The report aims to analyze the result and the characteristics of 2010 Changchun International Auto Expo, with a view to improving the organization of the event in the future. The Auto Expo is the largest event in Northeast China.

Findings

Held at the Changchun International Expo Center from July 14, 2010, the investigation indicates that the show was generally good, and it showed the following features.

♦ **Wide Participation**

2010 Changchun International Auto Expo attracted 50 types of name brand cars. Local Changchun large enterprises all attended the exhibition as the hosts. The size of the exhibition was massive, with many types of new cars gathered together.

♦ **Environment-friendly Subject**

Oil-saving and environment-friendly was the subject of this auto show. Because of the high international oil price and the potential green house effect, all exhibitors took advantage of 2010 Changchun International Auto Expo in demonstrating diesel and many other types of new energy models.

♦ **Sale-focused Arrangement**

Manufacturers, and distributors, were in the different halls. The sale characteristics of automobile were obvious. This arrangement fully showed that the sale of automobiles in Changchun Auto Show was close to market share.

♦ **Spot Instruction and Service**

The layout of the exhibition hall of Changchun International Auto Expo was rather complex. Therefore, the organizer of the exhibition had designed many guides to help visitors locate the exact of their interest. However, some visitors complained that the services were not personalized enough to cater to their needs.

Conclusions

Overall, it was concluded that 2010 Changchun International Auto Expo was successful, and the exhibitors were satisfied with the benefits from the show. However, some parts of the service need improving.

Recommendations

It is proposed that Changchun International Auto Expo should provide many convenient services for the visitors including stocking place, manuals and an information desk.

Vocabulary

investigation	[ɪnˌvestɪˈgeɪʃn]	n.	调查
characteristic	[ˌkærəktəˈrɪstɪk]	n.	特性
feature	[ˈfiːtʃə(r)]	n.	特征；特色
massive	[ˈmæsɪv]	adj.	广泛的

diesel	['diːzl]	n.	柴油；柴油机
manufacturer	[ˌmænjuˈfæktʃərə(r)]	n.	厂商
distributor	[dɪˈstrɪbjətə(r)]	n.	经销商
layer	[ˈleɪə(r)]	n.	层；阶层；地层
complex	[ˈkɒmpleks]	adj.	复杂的；合成的
aspect	[ˈæspekt]	n.	方面；方向
stock	[stɒk]	v.	储存
manual	[ˈmænjuəl]	n.	手册；指南

Notes

1. Changchun International Auto Expo 长春国际汽车博览会

2. The report aims to analyze the result and the characteristics of 2010 Changchun International Auto Expo, with a view to improving the organization of the event in the future.
   本报告旨在分析2010年长春国际汽车博览会的成果和特点，着眼于今后如何改进此类活动的组织。

3. 2010 Changchun International Auto Expo attracted 50 types of name brand cars.
   2010年长春国际汽车博览会吸引了50种名牌汽车参展。

4. Oil-saving and environment-friendly was the subject of this auto show.
   节能和环保是本次车展的主题。

5. Because of the high international oil price and the potential green house effect, all exhibitors took advantage of 2010 Changchun International Auto Expo in demonstrating diesel and many other types of new energy models.
   由于国际高油价和潜在的温室效应，所有参展商利用2010年长春国际汽车博览会展示柴油和许多其他类型的新能源车型。

6. The layout of the exhibition hall of Changchun International Auto Expo was rather complex.
   长春国际汽车博览会展馆的布局是相当复杂的。

Answer the following questions.

1. What are the characteristics of 2010 Changchun International Auto Expo?
2. What subject did the Expo focus on?
3. What was special about the arrangement of the Expo?
4. What did the visitors complain about?

Decide whether the following statements are True or False based on the above passage.

1. Changchun International Auto Expo is the largest event in China. ( )
2. Local Changchun enterprises all attended the exhibition as the hosts. ( )
3. The size of the show was massive, with many types of new cars gathered together. ( )
4. Manufacturers, and distributors, were in the different halls. ( )
5. The layout of the exhibition hall of Changchun International Auto Expo was rather simple. ( )
6. Some visitors complained that the services were not personalized enough to cater to their needs. ( )

Exercises

1. Match the words on the left with their proper meaning on the right.

(1) measure   a. someone who markets merchandise
(2) maximize   b. make as big or large as possible
(3) calculate   c. large formal assembly
(4) revenue   d. the act of presenting something to sight or view
(5) investment   e. make familiar or conversant with
(6) acquaint   f. money that is invested
(7) demonstration   g. the entire amount of income
(8) convention   h. make a mathematical calculation
(9) instruction   i. message describing how something is to be done
(10) distributor   j. evaluate the quality, or significance of

2. Read the following statements, and fill in the blank spaces with the appropriate words contained in the word box.

| customers   feedback   enhance   return   lead   financial |

(1) There are a number of ways to measure the _____ on investment for your efforts.
(2) The obvious objective for trade show exhibiting includes hard numbers such as _____ generation.
(3) _____ measures are essential for all marketing or sales strategies.